LUNAR &
BIODYNAMIC
GARDENING

LUNAR & BIODYNAMIC GARDENING

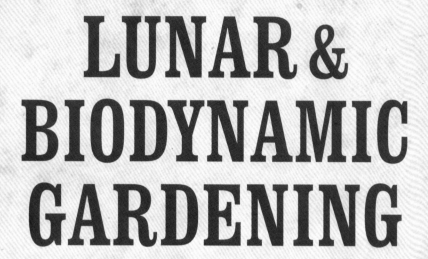

**PLANTING YOUR BIODYNAMIC GARDEN
BY THE PHASES OF THE MOON**

MATT JACKSON

CICO BOOKS
LONDON NEW YORK

Published in 2015 by CICO Books
An imprint of Ryland Peters & Small Ltd
20–21 Jockey's Fields   341 E 116th St
London WC1R 4BW   New York, NY 10029

www.rylandpeters.com

10 9 8 7 6 5 4 3 2 1

Artwork on page 9 and some step-by-step
photography by Matt Jackson

Artworks on pages 14 and 15 by Stephen Dew

A CIP catalog record for this book is available
from the Library of Congress and the British
Library.

ISBN: 978 1 78249 188 0

Printed in China

Editor: Caroline West
Designer: Mark Latter
Photographer: David Merewether

In-house editor: Dawn Bates
Art director: Sally Powell
Production controller: Mai-Ling Collyer
Publishing manager: Penny Craig
Publisher: Cindy Richards

For Laura: thank
you for bringing
happiness to
every day.

Additional photos
pages 3, 4, 11, 32, 33: istockphoto
pages 6, 8, 9: shutterstock
pages 134 br, 136, 137, 138, 139 br,
141, 143 br, 144, 146, 148, 150 bl,
151 br: Amanda Darcy

Contents

Introduction

This is a book about the most natural way to garden. Even more natural than "organic" gardening, lunar (moon) and biodynamic gardening both follow traditions that were practiced for over 10,000 years, but almost lost to us because of several centuries of mechanization and industrialization. These are not only methods for gardening, but also ways in which to live that are connected with Nature on a fundamental level and in tune with natural law.

∧ I've applied biodynamic principles to my own garden. This book charts my experiences and results.

This book focuses on two linked, but distinctly different, approaches to gardening. Both methods are rooted in our ancestral past, and predate scientific understanding, but have been developed and enhanced throughout the 20th century using modern knowledge and a healthy dose of hindsight. We have the ability to learn from our mistakes and to recognize the successes of millennia in our ever-evolving relationship with all life on Earth.

This book is an open-armed introduction to moon and biodynamic gardening for beginners. There are various reference books that go into great detail on the subjects of moon and biodynamic gardening, but there is really very little material available for the newcomer. I hope the book can fulfill this role and provide a reliable guide for gardeners just starting out on their lunar and biodynamic journey. When you have finished reading the book, I truly hope you will be inspired to dig deeper, which is why you will find a detailed Resources section on page 156 that will open up a wealth of understanding.

I personally discovered gardening in this way after a long career of over 20 years as a professional gardener. I started out initially by setting up a gardening round as a teenager in the sleepy Cornish town of Wadebridge, England. I grew up on my parents' little farm on Bodmin Moor and spent my formative years surrounded by Nature. My future path was fixed when I was taken on by the National Trust as a trainee gardener at Antony House, in Cornwall, where I learned every detail of modern, professional horticulture. It was also at this point in time that my connection with Nature became skewed and damaged, as I learned about chemicals such as herbicides, pesticides, and fungicides. I discovered how you could easily kill that which was in your way and lace the soil with a whole range of synthetic additives in order to make it "better" and turn it into a "healthy" environment for growing plants. I very soon forgot my childhood understanding of Nature and became caught up in a world of conquering, control, and manipulating Nature by force.

Setting up a small garden from scratch can be a steep learning curve, but quickly provides some wonderful results.

So what brought about the change?

My gardening path has taken me to some wonderful places: first as a gardener at Stourhead, in Wiltshire, then as a supervisor at the Oxford University Botanic Gardens, before becoming Head Gardener at Scotney Castle, in Kent. I have always questioned tasks, wanting to understand why I do them and to what end, and it was at Oxford that I first began to question so-called gardening tradition. However, my questioning approach could not be fully exercised until I became a Head Gardener.

I acquired another role as Head Gardener at Doddington Place, also in Kent, before becoming Gardens and Estate Manager at the world-famous Sissinghurst Castle. I joined as a new, large-scale vegetable garden of 2.2 acres (0.9 hectares) was in its fourth year, but struggling to succeed and in danger of closure. It was then that I asked Charles Dowding, a market gardener for 30 years, for advice. Charles has developed his own tried-and-tested style of organic growing called no-dig gardening, which is a highly productive, unmechanized way of growing fantastic vegetables, and the great thing is that this approach can also be applied to ornamental gardening.

I was very soon convinced that this was the right path for Sissinghurst Castle. So, we set about a rapid conversion, which saw year five yielding the best produce yet in far greater volumes. It also took me one giant step closer to Nature and being in tune with what plants really want, because in truth they only look to us for a bit of help.

It was moving to a new house, and a chance conversation with a friend that led me to pursue gardening by the phases of the moon and then on to biodynamics. I moved to an old oast house, historically used for drying hops for beer making, which is located on a farm in Kent. We were just at the end of the wettest winter on record, and the clay soil at my feet was waterlogged. My basic, but fair-sized, garden was to be a new project piece, and I knew that it would be no-dig, but my friend also mentioned moon gardening and this got me thinking.

A life-changing experience

Moon gardening soon led to biodynamics, so I paid a visit to Tablehurst Biodynamic Farm in East Sussex. I can only say that the experience had a profound effect on me: while walking around the farm, I became subconsciously aware that this was a special place and that everything around me was happy and content. Farm cats, pigs, horned cows, and people alike all brimmed with a relaxed contentment and obvious health.

When I finally reached the vegetable grounds, I found the fullest, greenest, healthiest lettuces growing beside many other first-class specimens. Tablehurst Farm convinced me of the benefits of biodynamics and some very helpful gardeners set me on the right path to becoming a lunar and biodynamic gardener.

My research has shown that there is little clarity on these methods of gardening for the beginner, while there are also many different variations put forward by a range of experienced gardeners. This book charts my experience of setting up a small garden from scratch in one season, as well as how I adopted biodynamic principles. It is full of practical examples and helpful tips for the beginner, while also being a useful resource for experienced traditional gardeners.

I don't claim it to be an exhaustive work on the intricacies of moon gardening and biodynamics, and remain humbled by the skill and wisdom of other gardeners with decades of experience. However, I hope it serves as a bridge that will bring you over to a place where the grass is very definitely greener.

My Garden Plan

I chose a small area at the side of the house to start a vegetable patch. I began by doing this sketch to work out what I wanted to grow.

With careful planning, and sketching what you'd like to achieve, you will grow more and have better results. *See Chapter 2, Getting Started, pages 34–57.*

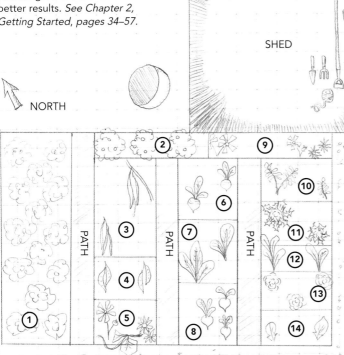
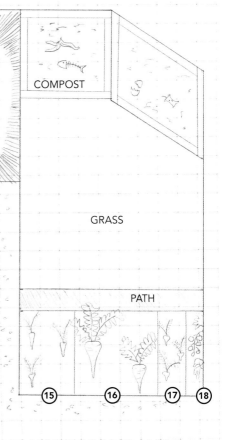

1 POTATOES 'NICOLA'

2 RUNNER BEANS

3 FRENCH BEANS

4 SUGAR PEAS (MANGETOUT)

5 COSMOS, CALENDULA, AND NASTURTIUM

6 BEETROOT (GOLD)

7 SWISS CHARD

8 BEETROOT (RED)

9 COSMOS, CALENDULA, AND BASIL

10 ROCKET

11 LETTUCE

12 PURPLE CHARD

13 LETTUCE

14 SPINACH

15 CARROTS 'NANTES' FOLLOWED BY WINTER SALAD

16 PARSNIPS

17 CARROTS 'BAMBINO' FOLLOWED BY WINTER SALAD

18 TOMATO AND BASIL

CHAPTER 1

Lunar Gardening and Biodynamics: The Basics

On first consideration, both lunar (moon) and biodynamic gardening can seem specialized and shrouded in mystery. However, this could not be further from the truth, with the methods involved in both approaches to gardening being natural and instinctive. In this chapter, I explain the key differences between moon gardening and biodynamic practices. I outline what's involved for you as a gardener when adopting these methods, how to work the soil, and how to use a lunar calendar to help you sow, plant, grow, and harvest in tune with the moon and stars. Finally, I talk about the results and benefits you can expect to achieve, whether you decide to adopt biodynamic gardening wholeheartedly or choose to distil your own version from the available information, as many gardeners do.

How It Works: Organic, Moon, and Biodynamic Gardening

There are many ways in which to garden, and we can be forgiven for thinking that the modern methods of intensive digging, chemical spraying, and artificial feeding are traditional, finely honed ones that we should follow. However, many of these supposedly traditional techniques were developed as part of the Agricultural Revolution (of the 18th and 19th centuries). In truth, for millennia, mankind has followed other influences—including working harmoniously with Nature, gardening by the moon, and using biodynamic methods—which we have since lost touch with, only for these to be reawakened in the 20th century and practiced by a few.

Organic gardening

Organic gardening has moved out of the shadows in recent decades and is now not only widely accepted, but also sought after and respected. Although still in the minority, many gardeners strive to achieve organic standards and, in fact, "go organic" is often the first piece of advice given to novice gardeners. Indeed, gardening organically is wonderful and is the first important step toward following the moon and introducing biodynamic methods.

The way in which we care for our gardens is essential in influencing how our plants respond because, although they are clever and will make the best of any situation, they are fixed to the spot where we have planted them and can only work with the conditions they have. For this reason, gardening organically is an essential starting-point for any would-be lunar or biodynamic gardener, as lunar gardening involves embracing Nature at a molecular level and every action you take will have an impact. Please don't be put off if you are a novice, however, because gardening organically is just a way to garden and must be learned in the same way as the conventional method of sloshing chemicals everywhere. In fact, I think organic gardening is an easier method to learn because with a well-balanced approach your natural instincts will quickly come to the fore.

When gardening organically, I advise a loose and flexible approach. Following the guidelines supplied by official certifying bodies can limit the real sensibilities of gardening at home, as they have been set up to provide standards for large-scale production and, in fact, often rule out the use of natural tonics and methods that cannot be measured scientifically. If you are in any doubt on how to proceed, ask yourself some simple questions: "What would happen in Nature?" "Is it more natural to apply an 'organic' feed that is made up of a concentration of ingredients or to add some balanced, well-rotted garden compost or manure?" "Can there really be such a thing as an 'organic' pesticide?" It's this level of awareness that will lead you along the right path when gardening by the moon and moving on to biodynamic gardening. Needless to say, if you have gardened organically up until this point, you are one step ahead, while if you are starting a garden from scratch, then you will find useful help and advice on getting started in the following chapters.

< By choreographing our lives with the natural world, we can all benefit in the garden, as we are the only ones that often work against it.

∨ All life in our gardens is influenced by the moon, including plants and gardeners as they toil to maintain them.

Moon gardening

It is quite common to confuse moon gardening with biodynamic gardening, and many people believe that they are one and the same thing. Although rooted in the same foundations that recognize the influence of the moon as significant over all life on Earth, they are, in fact, quite different. However, both methods take an entirely organic approach as a base level and then extend the nature of organic gardening to a more purified level.

The power of the moon over life on Earth is evident to us all, even in subtle ways. Very few people can ignore the draw of a great, luminescent full moon on a clear night, which brings out an instinctive and deep inner respect and appreciation. That same moon is the cause of unstoppable tides and creates great natural wonders such as the huge tidal range of the Severn Estuary in England. It is also responsible for the reproductive and menstrual cycles of many mammals. So, it is of little surprise that its gravitational pull also influences the movement of water through the soil, plants, and seeds—everything that exists on Earth, in fact. This means that any location where you garden will respond to the influence of the moon accordingly, whether this is a balcony terrace or a country estate, a simple potted tomato on a windowsill or an ornate French vegetable potager.

The moon's phases

The moon moves through four key stages in a lunar month. Moon gardeners track the phases of the moon as it orbits the Earth. In simple terms, this involves following the waxing and waning moon as it moves through its cycle to work out the best times to undertake different tasks in the garden. The sequence below shows the phases of the moon in the Northern Hemisphere.

WAXING CRESCENT   HALF MOON

First Quarter

WAXING GIBBOUS   FULL MOON

Second Quarter

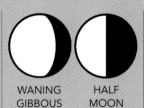

WANING GIBBOUS   HALF MOON

Third Quarter

WANING CRESCENT   NEW MOON

Fourth Quarter

THE PHASES OF THE MOON

Following a 28-day cycle, through an elliptical orbit, the moon has four quarters, which you'll need to be aware of when moon gardening. In the first quarter, it grows (waxes) from almost nothing, through a crescent, to a half moon. The second quarter sees it continue to grow (waxing gibbous) into a rich, full moon, before entering the third quarter. The next two phases see the moon shrink again (waning gibbous) to a half moon and then to a crescent (waning crescent) in the fourth quarter. It is these phases that are the easiest to see, understand, and work by when gardening. A growing, waxing moon (i.e. a moon that is getting bigger) has an opposing effect on the strength of Earth's own gravitational pull, resulting in water being drawn up into plants, seeds, and leaves. This means that a waxing moon, particularly in the second quarter of this phase, with its strong pull on water, is the best time to sow seed for optimum germination.

Earth's daily cycle

There is a daily cycle too: Earth's inhalation and exhalation, which recognizes that the Earth exhales and inhales at different times of the day. In the morning, the Earth exhales and releases its influence over water, thereby allowing sap to rise. Later in the day, the Earth inhales and draws sap down into plant roots and soil. So, how does this affect how we garden? In brief, lettuce will be plump and full in the morning, and more likely to wilt on picking in the evening. Conversely, a carrot will have more moisture and flavor if it is harvested in the evening.

FOLLOWING THE MOON'S PHASES

Moon gardeners closely track the phases of the moon as it orbits the Earth. They do this by following the phases on a moon calendar (see *Moon Calendars*, pages 20–23). Put simply, a basic approach to moon gardening involves following the waxing and waning moon to work out the best times to undertake different tasks in the garden. For example, a waning moon, which has less gravitational pull, is a good time for watering plants and feeding the soil because the water and feeds are more easily absorbed. There are many who believe that there are also optimum times to sow leaf, root, flower, and fruit/seed crops, which not only affects their germination, but also the quality and quantity of the final yield (for more advice on what to do when sowing according to the moon, see *Planting and Sowing by the Moon*, pages 24–27).

The moon's path

The path the moon takes through the sky changes because its orbit is at an angle to the Earth's orbit around the sun, which means it is sometimes moving above or below Earth's orbital "line." Many moon gardeners believe that the moon's position in its orbit (i.e. whether it is an ascending or descending moon) has a direct effect on many garden tasks. For instance, a descending moon is a good time for transplanting seedlings and feeding the soil.

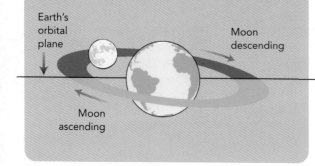

Earth's orbital plane

Moon descending

Moon ascending

There is, of course, a lot more to moon gardening than this, although a basic knowledge of the moon's phases is enough to start with. The process is further influenced by the planets, the stars, and our sun, as well as by variations in the moon's orbit (the path it takes around the Earth). However, my advice if you are just starting out in moon or biodynamic gardening is to work with these basic observations and use a moon or biodynamic gardening calendar that has been drawn up to achieve optimum results (see *Resources*, page 156).

Biodynamic gardening

Biodynamic gardening evolved throughout the 20th century and is still evolving now, as greater understanding develops. It originated in the teachings of Rudolf Steiner who, in a response to calls for help from German farmers in the 1920s, suggested ways in which to heal the soil. Farmers had noticed that the soil was suffering from the effects of intensive agriculture

(see page 18) and Steiner, working as both a scientist and spiritualist, blended earthly and terrestrial understanding to provide a method for repairing this damage. Steiner's advice was mostly based around using a number of special treatments—or "biodynamic preparations"—as well as ways in which to prepare them.

Steiner encouraged further research in the field, but sadly died before he could develop his teachings. However, many farmers and gardeners have gone on to study and progress his theories, including the late Maria Thun who linked the moon and the constellations to Steiner's teachings. Her work over decades researched, trialed, and perfected the process of sowing, planting, tending, and harvesting by the moon and the cosmos, which most calendars follow.

BIODYNAMICS—FIRST PRINCIPLES

Like moon gardeners, biodynamic gardeners closely follow the phases of the moon, as well as the alignments of the planets, stars, and our sun. However, this is neither the beginning nor the end of the biodynamic approach, as in its purest form it is also a holistic existence that looks at life in a different way and recognizes the farm or garden as a single living organism which is

A full "harvest" moon turns night into day, and has a powerful effect on plants, animals, and natural processes.

directly connected with, and powerfully related to, the moon, the planets, and the stars. In fact, so is everything that springs forth from the farm or garden—including us. We may have forgotten how to listen to this, but plants have not, and are completely in tune with the continual rhythms of Nature.

After centuries of a mechanical, chemical, and unnatural abuse of the land, biodynamics seeks to restore a harmonious natural state and its practitioners believe that a garden needs care and delicate management to keep it in healthy balance. Biodynamic gardeners understand that their role is to treat the soil well, to return to it what is missing, and to do this in a natural way. This healing and feeding process is achieved through the application of specially prepared tonics or biodynamic preparations, which act rather like homeopathic medicines, and provide the soil and plants with important trace elements. These preparations include BD 500 (Horn Dung Preparation) and BD 501 (Horn Quartz Preparation), among others (see pages 54–55). They were introduced by Steiner in 1924 and, despite being a little unusual in the way they are made, have scientifically proven positive results.

As you mix and prepare these biodynamic preparations, you bring conscious intent, or "mindfulness," to the gardening process, while also providing your garden with exactly what it needs. (For advice on making and using these preparations, see *Mixing and Using Biodynamic Preparations*, pages 74–5, and *The Biodynamic Compost Heap*, pages 76–9.) There is another benefit to using the preparations in that the healing process also makes the soil, which nourishes all plant life, more receptive to the subtle influences of the cosmos.

BIODYNAMICS—CONNECTING WITH YOUR GARDEN

While there is much to take in and think about, biodynamics is, in reality, a very practical way of working. The more you get involved, the more you get your hands grubby, the more you will connect with the soil, plants, and the entire garden organism. Indeed, by becoming the center of this activity, you will come to know your garden in an entirely different way and tune into the cycle of your plants. Good intentions are also essential as you start out on this gardening adventure. Much of lunar gardening—and all of biodynamics—requires this, because the energies your body creates all go into the mix.

So, where do you begin?

Firstly, you will need to decide at what level you would like to follow this natural approach to gardening. Do you want to be a moon or biodynamic gardener? The chart on the opposite page shows what is required to be an organic, moon, and biodynamic gardener. Whether you are a moon or biodynamic gardener, it really is worth sticking to a moon calendar, or you won't see the full effects of your efforts, and absolutely, and without question, you must garden organically. It is also worth pointing out that there are many gardeners who religiously follow the biodynamic path—and with truly wonderful results—but there are also others who distil their own blend to suit their lifestyle and are equally happy with the results.

It's easy to become bogged down in complexity, to be put off by words like biodynamic, and to feel bamboozled when reading about the moon, planetary alignments, ascending and descending moons, and a whole host of astronomical terms. However, gardening in this way is really quite simple, as well as instinctive once you have tuned in. As I've mentioned before, I think it helps to read and understand the theory, to immerse yourself in as much knowledge as possible, because you will then have a deep-rooted attachment to the process, even if you forget some of what you have learned.

The subsequent chapters in the book will help you through and provide plenty of detailed and practical advice to follow, while the *Resources* section will point you in the direction of further reading, training, and materials (see page 156). To summarize: with good soil, and the right plant material, you simply need to follow your moon calendar of choice, and enjoy the guaranteed benefits, whether of delicious produce or beautiful flowers.

Organic Gardening

Is rooted in low-impact horticulture and agriculture, using and working with Nature.

Calls for an environmentally friendly approach to gardening.

Promotes the harnessing of natural cycles and processes in the garden.

Demonstrates the importance of encouraging soil organisms to maintain healthy and fertile soil. This results in water-retentive soils that are rich in organic matter— and also healthy plants.

Uses organic matter (such as garden compost, well-rotted manure etc.) to create healthy soil in the belief that it is better to feed the soil than the plants.

Requires the use of organically sourced seed, garden compost, and other organic products, which are widely available.

Advocates good husbandry— providing plants early on with the right growing conditions and using good methods to care for them— in order to produce healthy, robust plants that are more resistant to shock and disease.

Biodynamic Gardening

Adheres stringently to organic principles as a starting-point for successful horticulture.

Like moon gardening, most biodynamic gardeners follow astrological timings to perform key garden tasks.

Acknowledges the vital importance of good soil and composting.

Recommends gardening with biodynamically grown seeds and plants.

Teaches the need to feed and "heal" the soil using specially prepared tonics. These biodynamic preparations and treatments provide the soil and plants with vital trace elements.

Regards the garden as a single living organism that should be sustained as a living whole.

Promotes a spiritual interaction between man, Nature, and the universe.

Calls on biodynamic practitioners to demonstrate mindfulness and a holistic approach to gardening.

Moon Gardening

Adheres to organic principles as a starting-point for horticulture.

Recognizes the influence of the moon on the growth and health of plants on Earth, as well as the activity of insects and animals, both friend and foe.

Acknowledges the effect of the sun, planets, and stars (as well as the moon) on all living things.

Advocates following the phases of the moon to decide the best times for tasks such as sowing, planting, harvesting, pruning, and grafting.

Follows an annual moon calendar to plan the best times to perform garden tasks.

Working the Soil

There are many theories on how best to work the soil, even within the biodynamic community, but by far the most sensible—and the one that I recommend—is that of not digging. The soil is so important to the health, vigor, and productivity of your garden that it must be treated with the utmost respect and care. It's precisely for this reason that I have dedicated a whole chapter to soil maintenance and the production of good garden compost.

Modern agriculture and gardening

Whether gardening by the moon or biodynamically, it is crucial that you adopt a holistic approach, starting with how you treat the soil in your garden. Since the moon, planets, and stars all generate influential energies, it is important that the soil is healthy if it is to act as a receptor of those energies. Sadly, for the last hundred years or so, agriculture and industry have covered the Earth with fertilizers, pesticides, and herbicides, significantly changing the makeup of the soil at a microscopic and elemental level. This is rather like applying a slightly caustic substance to your skin year after year until so much damage is done that help is needed to heal it. The result for Nature is stark. You need only walk into a field of wheat on a standard arable farm and it is dead apart from the crop. The soil is dry and lifeless, and the wheat entirely devoid of life, without a single insect or bird present. This is the result of a continual use of chemicals: herbicides to kill weeds, pesticides to kill insects, fungicides to kill molds, and fertilizers to replace everything that has been killed. In time, the soil structure is changed so much that it needs help to recover.

The no-dig approach

By not digging your soil, you consciously leave it alone to recover its structure and balance. A woodland floor provides a good model for how good soil can be created naturally in the garden. Every spring the woodland floor awakens and plants pop up, either as annuals or perennials, and then flower, seed, and die back. In this time, the trees leaf up, flower, seed, and then drop a fine mulch in the fall (autumn). This cycle takes place every year and the surface of the soil is covered in the softest and richest organic feed, which young plants love to seed into and perennials and woody plants to feed from. Below this light surface is a heavier, nutrient-rich, moisture-retentive soil, which further suits the plants, providing them with stability and durability in different climatic conditions. Over time, a rich, layered soil develops, and it is this that we emulate in our gardens by not digging. By only adding garden compost to the surface of the soil, we allow it to recover this layered structure, which will be teeming with life at the surface and ideal for growing garden plants.

Maintaining good soil

Good soil is of paramount importance—as is the ability to get hold of or make rich, healthy garden compost—whether you are an organic, moon, or biodynamic gardener (see *Chapter 3*).

You will need to maintain your soil with routine additions of organic garden compost, as well as special preparations if you decide to follow the biodynamic path.

∧ Rich, dark, and nutritious soil—the small, no-dig beds in this garden are frequently mulched with garden compost and have a perfect structure for healthy growth.

> An oasis of vibrant, organic growth, this garden was recovered from redundant agricultural land and brought to life with compost and first-class husbandry.

Healing the soil

As well as adopting a no-dig approach, Rudolf Steiner's teachings show how you can assist further by actively healing the soil. By identifying key trace elements in both the soil and in plants, Steiner suggested using healing tonics or biodynamic preparations made from entirely natural ingredients. These should be prepared in such a way that they are energized by the influence of the moon, planets, and stars.

It is the use of these preparations (see pages 54–5), in particular, that sets biodynamic gardening apart from organic gardening, which still employs some powerful concoctions that may harm the delicate balance of the soil. Indeed, even the use of approved "organic" fertilizers or pesticides, such as slug pellets, is not acceptable in the biodynamic garden since they also contribute to an imbalance in the soil.

Tools to keep your soil healthy

The following materials and tools will help you "work" your garden soil so that it is in tune with Nature:

* A good supply of well-made garden compost
* Some well-rotted animal manure, preferably cow manure, to be used from time to time
* A hoe, as this is the best way to combat weeds without damaging the structure of the soil
* A bucket, a watering can, rainwater, and biodynamic preparations to add to your garden

Moon Calendars

I have referred to moon or lunar calendars several times, as well as to the various sowing and planting days, so I think it's worth explaining the theories on which these are based. It is also worth mentioning that moon calendars can differ according to the information they are drawing on and whether you live in the Northern or Southern Hemisphere.

Whether you are moon or biodynamic gardening, you will need to follow a moon calendar. There are several available, but some are definitely more accessible for the novice. I like the *Lunar Organics* wall chart, but probably find Nicholas Kollerstrom's diary most useful in the garden (see *Resources*, page 156). I check the calendar most days, just to keep in tune with what's around the corner. I also have a phone app that keeps me up-to-date with the moon's phases. But, most of all, I often find myself outside at night, simply looking up at the sky with a different view of it all.

Moon phases
Initially, moon calendars detail the phases of the moon, month by month, so that you can see its progress through the year (see page 14). If you decide that you are only going to follow this monthly guide when planting, sowing, and harvesting, then the information is very clear. For example, it is best to sow seed when the moon is waxing and close to full, and to plant out when it is waning and close to new. Fruits and leaves will be fuller in a waxing moon, while root vegetables will be moist and tasty in a waning moon.

Moon paths
Moon calendars also give information in various ways on the moon's path, i.e. whether it is ascending or descending (see page 15). Some moon gardeners take note of the moon's path when planning garden tasks. For example, planting in a descending moon puts less stress on the roots of a young plant because the moon's pull on its sap is not as strong. Some gardeners do not place much importance on this information, but there are others who swear by it. Personally, I have seen it in the activity of slugs, which become prolific in an ascending moon path, especially during a full moon, and hide away during a descending new moon.

Elemental days
The next level of information on a typical moon calendar are the elemental days. These are referred to as root, leaf, flower, and fruit/seed days, and are grouped according to the Earth, Water, Air, and Fire elements of astronomical constellations. So, leaf days are associated with the element Water, root days with the element Earth, flower days with the element Air, and fruit/seed days with the element Fire. When looking at calendars such as these, you will notice that these constellations are linked to the star signs with which we are all familiar from the zodiac. For example, my water sign of Pisces is also a leaf sign. Three of these star signs are attributed to each element, as well as to different plant features: Earth and Root Days with Taurus, Virgo, and Capricorn; Water and Leaf Days with Pisces, Scorpio, and Cancer; Air and Flower Days with Gemini, Libra, and Aquarius; and Fire and Fruit/Seed Days with Aries, Sagittarius, and Leo.

If you are gardening according to these elemental days, then let them be your guide when deciding the best times to sow, plant, and harvest different types of crop. For example, aim to sow, plant, and harvest tomatoes, bell (sweet) peppers, eggplants (aubergines) on a fruit day and carrots, parsnips, and potatoes on a root day.

It is important to note here that moon calendars work to a different rule, being grounded in astronomy, not astrology—they therefore use the sidereal zodiac, not the tropical one. They are based on the science of the sky and help to pin-point more accurately the position of the moon in relation to the various stellar groupings. Many

> The sun is the engine of life on Earth and it is sunlight that the moon reflects. It is, therefore, not difficult to see that sun, moon, and stars have an influence when you begin to look.

moon gardeners believe that the effect of the moon on plant life is intensified as it passes in front of these astronomical constellations, a phenomenon that is also observed in biodynamic gardening.

Incidentally, it was Maria Thun who first noticed the influence of the stars on plant life and spent her life researching and refining this understanding. The planets in our own Solar System may feature on some moon calendars, as they also have a bearing on what happens here on Earth: so much so, in fact, that you will find days when you are advised not to enter the garden because it is not a good time to work it.

An important point to bear in mind is that the constellations are not the same size and the moon passes in front of them for differing lengths of time. It is in this respect that moon calendars can differ. The most accurate calendars, including the Maria Thun and *Lunar Organics* versions, recognize this fact and you will notice that the associated days vary in size as a result. This is the truly purist approach and used by committed biodynamic gardeners. Other moon calendars, such as that of Nicholas Kollerstrom, are a little simpler in that they divide the constellations equally, giving equal weight to the days, and are more in line with the practices of our ancestors. Essentially, it is your choice which moon calendar you decide to follow, but I personally look at several and work when they all agree.

I should point out that not all biodynamic gardeners follow the elemental days. I have worked alongside some very experienced gardeners who have devoted their lives to understanding Rudolf Steiner's teachings and they believe that biodynamics is all about soil care and good husbandry, with a healthy respect for the influences of the Solar System. They believe that this was the focus of Steiner, that he didn't highlight the astronomical constellations as important for a good reason, and that the biodynamic way is all about using the biodynamic preparations and practical land management.

How cosmic influences affect Earth

How the cosmos affects life on Earth is a complex science to understand, but relatively easy to put into context. We know our sun is a very powerful force, controlling the growth of plants and emitting strong radio waves. We know the moon has a significant impact, controlling the tides and the weather, but it also acts as a giant mirror that reflects sunlight back to the Earth at night. So, it stands to reason that with this light come radio waves, which have a greater effect when it is a full moon as opposed to a new moon. With this in mind, why shouldn't every planet in our Solar System, and every star that we can see, have a similar effect, however small that might be? These celestial bodies all produce some form of radio frequency, which is detectable from Earth with radio telescopes, and therefore have the potential to influence all life.

Moon Calendar Sample Month

A moon or biodynamic gardening calendar will help you work out the best times for sowing, planting, and harvesting crops, as well as for cultivating plants in the ornamental garden.

A typical moon calendar details the phases of the moon, month by month, as well as whether the moon is ascending or descending. It also identifies when the moon is passing in front of the 12 astronomical constellations (denoted by zodiac symbols), so giving rise to the optimum fruit/seed, flower, leaf, and root days (known as elemental days).

Moon calendars all give similar information, which can be presented in a number of different ways, but you will soon get used to the layout of the calendar you are using. At first, it can seem a little complicated, so use your moon calendar at a level you are comfortable with.

Opposite is what you can expect to see when you buy a typical moon calendar. It shows a sample month (June 2014) from a calendar for gardeners in the Northern Hemisphere. With all this information before you, it is easy to plan and organise a gardening month, working out optimum times, good times, and times to avoid various gardening tasks.

(For further advice on the best times for sowing, planting, and harvesting, *see Planting and Sowing by the Moon*, pages 24–7 and *Harvesting—Ideal Times*, pages 28–9.)

Key garden tasks by the moon

Your moon calendar will guide you on what to do when, but below are some optimum times to bear in mind for different gardening tasks.

WAXING MOON

* Sow leaf crops because water/energy is drawn upward into the leaves.

* Sow just prior to a full moon (in the second quarter) for the best germination of seed.

* Keep an eye out for slugs and snails, and remove them manually (this is best done at night).

* Harvest leaf crops in the morning on leaf days.

WANING MOON

* Sow root crops because water/energy is pulled down to the roots.

* Good for pruning, as sap is being drawn down.

* Cut wood for pea sticks and supports, as well as for burning.

* Feed the soil.

* Harvest root vegetables.

ASCENDING MOON

* During an ascending moon, the sap in plants is drawn up, so gardeners should harvest non-root crops.

* Sow seed, especially of above ground crops.

* Look out for snails and slugs.

* Take cuttings and graft plants.

DESCENDING MOON

* During a descending moon, the sap in plants is drawn down, so gardeners should plant or transplant seedlings, especially those of root crops.

* Hoe off weeds.

* Feed the soil.

* Prune.

* Mow the grass.

Sample month

1 SUN	2 MON	3 TUE	4 WED	5 THU	6 FRI	7 SAT	8 SUN
6 12 18	6 12 18	6 12 18	6 12 18	6 12 18	6 12 18	6 12 18	6 12 18
♊ Ⓐ			♌		Ⓑ	♍	

9 MON	10 TUE	11 WED	12 THU	13 FRI Ⓒ	14 SAT	15 SUN	16 MON
6 12 18	6 12 18	6 12 18	6 12 18	6 12 18	6 12 18	6 12 18	6 12 18
	♎		♏	04:12 ♐			♑

17 TUE	18 WED	19 THU	20 FRI	21 SAT	22 SUN	23 MON	24 TUE Ⓓ
6 12 18	6 12 18	6 12 18	6 12 18	6 12 18	6 12 18	6 12 18	6 12 18
	♒	♓		Summer Solstice	♈		♉

25 WED	26 THU	27 FRI	28 SAT	29 SUN	30 MON		
6 12 18	6 12 18	6 12 18	6 12 18	6 12 18	6 12 18 Ⓔ		
		♊					

A. Each day of the week is colored according to the elemental day (i.e. root, leaf, flower, fruit/seed days).

B. Some days have two colors because these are changeover days from one elemental day to the next.

C. The phase of the moon is given for each day. In this example, June 13 is a full moon.

D. The light and dark blue boxes above each calendar day indicate the moon's path (i.e. whether it is ascending or descending).

E. This part indicates at exactly what time the changeover between the elemental days takes place.

Key

MOON PHASES

- Waxing Moon
- Waning Moon
- New Moon
- Full Moon

MOON PATHS

- Ascending Moon Path
- Ascend/Descend Path Transition
- Descending Moon Path

ELEMENTAL DAYS

ROOT DAY

- ♉ Taurus
- ♍ Virgo
- ♑ Capricorn

Sow, plant, and harvest carrots, parsnips, turnips, radishes, beets (beetroot), rutabaga (swede), onions, garlic, and potatoes.

FLOWER DAY

- ♊ Gemini
- ♎ Libra
- ♒ Aquarius

Sow, plant, and harvest globe artichokes, as well as sow or plant annuals and perennials.

LEAF DAY

- ♓ Pisces
- ♏ Scorpio
- ♋ Cancer

Sow, plant, and harvest salads, brassicas, arugula (rocket), leafy herbs, Swiss and ruby chard. Also maintain lawns and hedges.

FRUIT/SEED DAY

- ♈ Aries
- ♐ Sagittarius
- ♌ Leo

Sow, plant, and harvest squashes, tomatoes, cucumbers, peppers, eggplants (aubergines), zucchini (courgettes), peas and beans, as well as tree fruits like apples and pears and soft fruits such as strawberries, raspberries, and blackberries.

Planting and Sowing by the Moon

Although an understanding of optimum planting and sowing times is the key to success in the vegetable garden, it may take you a few seasons working with the phases of the moon before it becomes an instinctive part of your gardening routine. For this reason, I recommend you obtain a moon calendar that is designed for this purpose (i.e. to give information on optimum planting and sowing times) and follow it rigidly. Be aware of what your calendar is detailing because it will tell you why it is a good day to carry out a certain garden task. Let the calendar lead you by the hand and trust it as you would a dear friend.

Lunar cycles and crop yields

There has been much research on how crops are affected by lunar cycles and the results are shockingly clear. The moon has a cycle of 18 years, which sees bumper crops at the end of each 18-year cycle, along with unusual weather events to match. Our sun has a 22-year sun spot cycle, which again sees peaks and troughs in crop yields on Earth. The reproduction of all animals can also be studied throughout history, with the same effects noted, especially in relation to a full moon versus a new moon, with maternity wards seeing higher birth rates at a full moon and two days either side. Added to this, the biodynamic movement has also spent 60 years trialing Steiner's theories and analyzing the results. This has led to convincing evidence that biodynamics is a system of gardening and agriculture that really works.

Deciding when to plant

Good planning is the key to gardening successfully according to the moon, but, to be honest, this is the same for any method of gardening. I have always worked to some form of calendar and schedule; it's just that now I'm being guided by the moon. If you look at each

< Deciding when to plant is important, as there are perfect times, good times, and bad ones. Be guided by your calendar until you feel confident enough to make your own judgements based on the different options.

month, or each moon phase, and plan the jobs ahead, marking on the calendar when you intend to plant, then you will not go wrong and will feel in perfect step.

For example, as I write this, I know that my tomato plants are ready to come out of their pots and find their feet in the garden. My moon calendar tells me that it is a fruit day until four o'clock, so today is an initial possibility. Looking more closely, however, I note that we are in an ascending moon, which pulls sap up. This will expect a lot from my young plants, which have yet to develop a strong root system, so I am far better to wait seven days, when the next descending moon is in a fruit sign. My plants are able to wait, and next week is convenient to me, but if it had to be today, then that would be fine. So, working with plants on the correct days is an ideal starting-point—and we should always aim for the optimum time—but sometimes a variation simply has to occur.

Deciding when to sow

The very same approach applies to seeds, but of particular influence here is the effect of a waxing gibbous moon. A great many studies have shown that the moisture uptake and subsequent germination of seeds reaches its peak several days before a full moon. Seed is, therefore, most likely to germinate quickly, consistently, and with vigor during this moon phase, making it an ideal time to sow. In addition to this, adhering to the correct elemental days

∧ Sowing seed just prior to a full moon will see the strongest germination.

∨ Sow and plant at the right time to achieve consistently high levels of success.

Better color, flavor, and storage capabilities are all qualities that can be expected from produce grown in a biodynamic garden.

afterward will further add to the final success of your plants. To give an example, looking at my lunar calendar for the next full moon, I can see that the two days before the full moon are leaf days, so this is the perfect time for sowing lettuce, spinach, and herbs, for example. However, in the week leading up to the full moon, there are also root and flower days, while the evening and day following the full moon are fruit days. This means that whatever crops I am planning to sow that month—whether these are leaf, root, flower, or fruit crops—I can be sure that they will be sown at the optimum time.

The key once again is being organized. All gardens should revolve around a plan, because it will help you keep on top of things, even if it changes a little throughout the season. With a plan, you can order your seed in advance, so getting the best prices and choices. Once you have your seed, spend an hour going through the packets, marking whether they are fruit, flower, leaf, or root crops, and then plan the best times to sow them.

Does it make a difference?

So why stick to the days? Why does it matter? Well, there is a very obvious reason and this is simply that you will get the best end results. Consistent trials have shown that the same crop sown on every single day of the month for several months sees remarkable differences. Sown on the correct days, the color, flavor, and size are perfect, and yet the very same seed, in the same soil, sown on the wrong day can be tasteless, pithy, stunted, oversized, or any combination of these poor qualities. Having tasted the results of a fully functioning biodynamic garden, I am in no doubt that the end product is worth the work.

Biodynamic seeds and plants

Seeds and plants will perform best if they have been gathered and raised with their roots in the biodynamic garden. Everything in a seed is stored energy and if gathered at the optimum time— from a plant grown in the optimum way—it will respond far better. Start as you mean to go on is perhaps the best first lesson (see *Seed*, pages 48–51).

> This Swiss chard has been raised from biodynamically produced seed. It therefore has the very best of everything at a molecular level and responds brilliantly to biodynamic husbandry.

Harvesting—Ideal Times

People often say to me: "The problem with growing vegetables is that there is nothing for ages and then an almighty glut of everything, which is too much to cope with." This really is a common occurrence, and I've made the same mistake as well, but with some careful thought it actually need not happen that way. When to harvest is not an exact science because the weather has such an effect but, with a little planning, it is possible to estimate what to expect.

∧ If lifted in the afternoon or evening, when the Earth is inhaling, root vegetables will be at their most succulent and full of flavor.

A glut in produce is usually the result of sowing too much seed initially. If you buy one type of green (French) bean, and sow the entire packet on the same day, then it stands to reason that it will fruit all at once, resulting in a glut of beans. However, if you sow a quarter of the packet once a month, then you will have a nicely spaced harvest. If you also combine this approach with the sowing of two different varieties of green bean, such as an early and a late, then you really will extend the season (see *Keeping Your Salad Bowl Full All Year*, pages 94–5).

Planning the sowing and planting dates is one thing, but knowing when to harvest is another. The taste test really is the best guide here until you become familiar and comfortable with your plants. I find it can be very easy to let something get past its best, with fresh young carrots becoming a little too "woody" or beans too stringy, so don't be afraid to pick early and taste first.

Following the lunar principle that the Earth exhales in the morning, allowing moisture to plump up foliage, followed by an inhalation in the afternoon that draws moisture down to the roots, we can make some informed harvesting decisions. For example, leafy produce such as lettuce will be turgid and tasty in the morning, keeping for longer when picked, whereas carrots, beets (beetroot), and new potatoes will be full of succulence and flavor in the afternoon.

Moon gardeners who follow the elemental signs believe that harvesting vegetables for storage on the correct day— that is, onions on a root day, salads on a leaf day, tomatoes on a fruit day, and so on—will ensure that they keep in better condition and hold their flavor for longer. This is less practical for non-storage produce, such as tomatoes and salads, which is best harvested fresh and when it is ready. The same principles can also be applied to cut flowers, whereby flowers arranged indoors keep far better after being cut on a flower day.

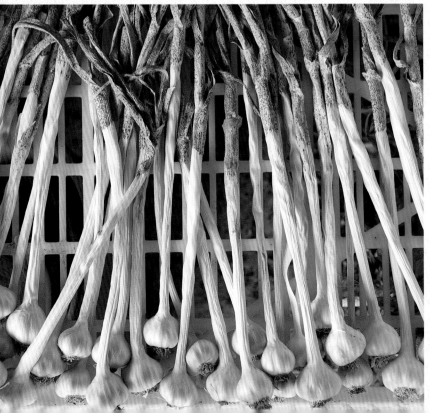

∧ Picking lettuce in the morning, as the Earth exhales, ensures that they will be full of water and store for longer.

< Gathering garlic on the afternoon of a descending moon, and also on a root day if this is possible, will make for better long-term storage.

29

The Results—What to Expect

Whether you choose to garden by following the moon or biodynamic principles you can expect to have a very different outlook on gardening. I have personally found that I have a much greater awareness of what is going on around me. I know what the moon is doing and what to expect from the weather. I also notice the wildlife in my garden in a different way. I think your senses change a little and that you become less fixated on individual issues, noticing more subtle trends and needs in your garden.

As a biodynamic gardener, I have gardened without a thought for using any chemicals, whether in the form of fertilizers or pest and disease killers. I didn't use many chemicals before, but knowing that even "organic" slug pellets are out has given me a liberated feeling. I have had very few problems with weeds or pests, as a result of good husbandry, and have produced some very delicious vegetables. I feel as though I have a personal relationship with my plants, as if I know them as individuals, and so have a changed level of care for them.

I have also been impressed with what I grow, but the real proof is to be found at flourishing organic and biodynamic farms and gardens, such as Tablehurst Farm, East Sussex, and Homeacres, Somerset, both of which are in England, where I have eaten perhaps the best-tasting vegetables ever. These were so full of flavor and made me feel good inside. Being able to create a garden in this manner and to feel so aware of one's natural surroundings is a marvelous experience and a way of life that you can expect to have if you garden in this way.

Abundance, health, and happiness for plants, animals, and humans can all be achieved in natural, biodynamic gardens.

Ornamental gardens thrive when tended according to lunar and biodynamic principles, becoming a haven for wildlife all year.

Rural Edible Garden

Dan Kijowski and his partner Maria Harding garden a small piece of paradise called Hazelrowan Wood, near Totnes, Devon, in South West England. They have worked this ¾-acre (0.3-hectare) site, which is made up of south-facing terraces, for two years, having spent a year clearing it first. The site has a clay-loam soil with a pH of 6.5.

Dan has a background as a musician, but always had an interest in gardening. A change in direction saw him volunteering on organic farms and market gardens for several years before starting his own enterprise. He is entirely self-taught, having developed his knowledge from his time spent volunteering, as well as learning from successes and failures. Dan's first major influence was Bob Flowerdew, but he has recently found Charles Dowding (see pages 112–3) to be his main guide, liking his logical approach.

Dan regards his gardening style as low impact, respectful of nature, and sustainable. He practices no-dig gardening, using no machinery, and is entirely organic. He also manages to supply 66lb (30kg) of salad a week to local customers, along with some surplus vegetables.

As far as possible Dan follows the Maria Thun calendar for sowing and also aims to time this task with a full moon. He likes the order that this brings, the opportunity to plan ahead, and also the time to focus positive intent on the

Dan's wonderful terraced garden, showing the narrow no-dig beds at various stages.

process. He is less rigid about planting and harvesting times, but follows a moon calendar where practical.

So, what drives him? The pay is poor, it's hard work, and there can be failures, but Dan enjoys the positivity of self-sufficiency, non-reliance, and the social benefits of gardening naturally.

> A simple, modest polytunnel provides enough protected space to raise everything for this large garden.

∧ Space for unusual varieties—these purple French beans add interest to the garden and kitchen.

> A range of lettuce growing to the tune of the moon, in beautiful, organic soil.

"I function well outdoors, and it is good for my mental wellbeing."

CHAPTER 2

Getting Started

Starting on a new project can be the hardest step to take, especially if you are faced with an unworked garden or an overgrown allotment. It can seem all the more daunting if you are a gardening novice. However, the truth is that gardening is not as hard as it may at first seem, whichever method you choose to practice, and the rewards for the physical effort you put in are immeasurable. I have yet to meet a gardener who does not get a deep sense of satisfaction from his or her work, and this satisfaction is even more profound for organic gardeners. All you need to clear that first hurdle is some basic knowledge, a sound plan, and the right materials. No garden is ever too small or too large, and you will discover that lunar and biodynamic knowledge can be applied anywhere, with a range of variations to suit all gardeners.

Your Space—What You Can Achieve

Your garden may consist of a single window box, a sumptuous balcony, a yard filled with fertile troughs and raised beds, or a garden so large that you need outside help to care for it. Whatever type of space you have, it can be rewarding, beautiful, productive, and food for the soul. It is surprising what can be achieved with careful thought and good planning. I have at times been astonished by the productivity of some very small spaces, as well as envious of people with large, diverse, and well-worked gardens.

Whether you are starting a garden from scratch or adapting to a new way of gardening, it is important to start with a plan. Consider these simple questions:

* HOW DO YOU WANT TO USE YOUR SPACE?
* WHEN WILL YOU USE IT?
* HOW MUCH TIME DO YOU WISH TO COMMIT?
* HOW MUCH MONEY DO YOU WANT TO SPEND?
* DO YOU KNOW WHAT YOU'RE DOING?

∧ Borlotti beans have beautifully marbled pods, making them a highly decorative feature in a productive garden. Borlotti beans are ideal in salads and casseroles.

The answers to these questions will guide you when planning your garden, influencing how you lay it out, what you choose to grow, and whether you need help or not. The most important piece of advice I can offer is to keep the garden simple to start with. The smaller the space, the more pertinent this advice becomes, and the same can be said of the time you have available to tend your garden. You may, for example, have a balcony, only 15 minutes to spare per day, and a desire to eat something you've grown. The easiest way to get started is to grow some salad leaves all season, following the lunar cycles (see Chapter 1) at each stage, and ensuring through repeat sowings that you always have something to crop. By doing this, you will definitely have the best salads you have ever eaten, which are ready to pick the moment they are needed.

Once you have decided what you would like to achieve, you will need to plan your garden. It is important to measure it, draw it out to scale, and then sketch in what you hope to grow (see my garden plan on page 9). While doing this you can also check the recommended planting distances for your chosen plants, how long the plants will be in the ground, how much seed or how many plants you need to buy, and what you might expect to achieve at the end. With this in mind you will grow in confidence, be able to plan a calendar of work, and enjoy the best bit—getting your hands dirty and growing plants.

With careful planning much can be grown, and in large gardens a whole range of things, from flowers to vegetables.

My garden

To put these thoughts into context, I thought it might be useful to describe my own garden, which I started from scratch at the same time as writing this book. I have a reasonably large lawn, adjacent to arable fields, which is where I first planned to make a vegetable garden. However, I soon changed my mind when I realized how heavily the crops were sprayed and fertilized. So, instead, I chose a small area at the side of my house, which is well protected from the farming activities and in a sheltered, sunny spot.

The area measures 26ft by 10ft (8m by 3m), with an adjacent shed and composting area. I regard this as a small garden, typical of many gardens and yards in urban settings, and a good example of just what can be achieved. I have no glasshouse, direct sowing all of the seed outdoors or sowing it in cells to be transplanted later as young plants. I also started my new vegetable garden by mulching the ground only (see page 65) and adhering to a no-dig approach (see pages 64–5).

In this small area I grew a range of root, fruit, flower, and leaf crops, as well as some ornamental flowers for insects and pure prettiness. The edible crops included:

* POTATOES
* RUNNER BEANS
* GREEN (FRENCH) BEANS
* SUGAR PEAS (MANGETOUT)
* BEETS (BEETROOT)
  –GOLDEN AND RED VARIETIES
* SWISS CHARD
* PURPLE CHARD
* TOMATOES
* SALAD LEAVES
* SPINACH
* ARUGULA (ROCKET)
* PARSNIPS
* CARROTS

∧ Purple chard with its red-veined leaves looks highly attractive in the vegetable garden. It is also bountiful and great to cook with.

∨ Young mangetout peas start to climb natural pea sticks, with Cosmos nearby for flower.

Moon gardening on a small scale

Gardening by the moon can be achieved at any level, even in the smallest of containers, since plants do not stop responding to the universe in which they live. Some of the biodynamic preparations can be used in quite small areas, although adopting the system fully becomes easier when you can have a compost heap to complete the cycle.

Small Spaces

This type of garden space probably needs the most careful consideration, as every inch counts, although a lot can be achieved with a good plan. By small spaces, I mean balconies, courtyards, and small gardens of up to 200 square feet (24 square meters)—in other words, any area that can be cared for with basic hand tools alone. Many of these spaces, including windowsills, balconies, and courtyards, will focus purely on gardening in containers.

< Small spaces, with careful planning, can contain lots of plants. With its perennial border and floral frame this courtyard still has plenty of room for pots and planters full of vegetables or annuals, and a long season of interest.

To garden successfully in a small space, good planning and close adherence to a moon calendar are fundamental. Keeping everything simple will make the project far better. In this instance, sticking to the old adage that it is better to do several things incredibly well, rather than a lot of things badly certainly holds true.

When planning how to grow in such a space, consider what is most important to you and work from there. You may like the thought of growing a range of vegetables, but a balcony might only lend itself to two or three types. However, it is surprising what you can achieve in a small space. For example, I once had a small shaded greenhouse, measuring only 6ft by 3ft (1.8m by 1m), in which I was able to grow salad leaves that lasted from spring until winter, two batches of sugar peas (mangetout), chili peppers, and tomatoes that lasted all summer, which was enough to produce 10 pints (5.6 liters) of homemade sauces for freezing. So, there is no reason why a well-positioned balcony cannot provide the same sort of crops or a rich and vibrant display of colorful and fragrant flowers all season.

Being biodynamic

How do we fit moon cycles and biodynamic practices into such small areas? The effects of the moon are felt everywhere, in the smallest of corners, and so will work perfectly well in confined situations. However, it is trickier to be fully biodynamic in a small space, which is rooted in diversity and a connection to real soil (as opposed to potting media). For this reason, small spaces at the larger end of the scale will better accommodate a biodynamic approach because it can be difficult to obtain

really good growing media if you are using containers. (Growing in containers is dealt with specifically in Chapter 6: *Pots and Containers*, pages 134–53). Another good option is to use the Mausdorf Starter (see page 78) in all potting media when potting up plants, the starter also being suitable for watering on.

However, biodynamic preparations are easy to prepare and use in the smallest of spaces, and your plants will respond well to them wherever they are growing. For example, applying BD 500 to the soil or planters will only improve the growing conditions, while spraying BD 501 on your plants will also improve their health and vigor. If you have enough space for a compost heap of any size, then you can begin to make biodynamic garden compost (see *The Biodynamic Compost Heap*, pages 76–9) and be on the road to great things.

∧ You can grow a wide range of produce in just one square meter of garden. These planters contain some common herbs, ornamental Cosmos, Nasturtium, and Calendula, mixed salads, and two varieties of tomato.

Medium Spaces

The larger the garden, the more physical work is required for maintenance, but the range of opportunities also begins to soar. For a beginner, progressing to a garden of this size (60ft/18m long and 15ft/5m wide, for example) can be quite daunting, especially if you've only previously had a balcony, but don't be alarmed as there are easy methods for starting out small and simple.

∧ Here, an area of lawn has been left to grow longer, with the clover providing nectar. The grass beyond is longer still and provides a diverse habitat for wildlife.

Medium-sized gardens have the benefit of being more open to the sky and are therefore exposed to everything that this gives us, including rain, wildlife, and solar or lunar rays. There is usually a good depth of soil, or space for large raised beds, making it possible to create rich and nutritious growing conditions. Of significant importance is the opportunity to include a compost heap, which is vital when gardening organically and biodynamically.

As with small spaces, a plan is really important, so ask yourself the same questions when you are planning gardening activities from scratch or with future changes in mind. You might decide to start off on a small scale by working only one area intensively to grow edible plants, for example. If your garden is laid down to lawn, then this is a good way to simplify maintenance at the beginning. Mowing once a week, or fortnightly, not only keeps the lawn tidy, but the grass cuttings will also provide valuable additions for the compost heap. However, long grass creates a good habitat for a range of beneficial insects and mammals, not only providing shelter, but also nectar and seeds. So, you may wish to leave the grass to grow long, cutting it only once in mid-summer or early fall (autumn), and then a second time in mid-fall. As your experience grows and your plans develop, you will be able to reduce the size of your lawn or meadow, gradually turning it into vegetable or ornamental beds.

Special features

Gardens of this size broaden the range of features you can include, such as ornamental areas and play zones, as well as providing an opportunity to keep bees and chickens, and grow fruit and a wide range of vegetables. Primarily, I would allow space for a compost heap, positioned conveniently for adding to and emptying. Having said that, you may wish to tuck it behind a shed or trellis screen. Not essential, but of benefit early in the growing season, is a small glasshouse, lean-to propagation frame, or cold frame, as these enable you to get seedlings going just a bit earlier than open-sown seed.

How you work and care for your soil is also an important decision when planning your garden. These days I recommend only a no-dig approach to gardening. Although many traditional gardeners find it difficult to have faith in this system and new gardeners discover that there is little support for it, there are, in fact, many gardeners—from domestic enthusiasts to professional growers—who adopt this way of doing things and find they can grow better plants in far less time and with less heavy labor. By gardening in this way, you can achieve almost everything in a medium-sized garden with only hand tools, a wheelbarrow, and an organized approach.

Here, too, biodynamic gardening can become a fully workable system, in which natural diversity and contact with terra firma provide the foundations for plants to benefit from improved soil, the use of the biodynamic preparations, and the application of biodynamic garden compost.

∧ This bright, open space with its pretty existing border is ideal for a gradual, phased development.

A large garden allows for a wide range of options. Charles Dowding's garden has a large greenhouse that produces vegetables all year round.

Large Spaces

Large gardens are the perfect environment for establishing a fully biodynamic ecosystem, allowing for a range of diverse habitats, while also providing a good buffer against surrounding artificial activities and lifestyles. In a large garden you can grow vegetables all year round, have a designated area for fruit, and enjoy ornamental planting schemes as well.

The larger garden provides ample space for those all-important compost heaps, along with sheds, glasshouses, polytunnels, chickens, orchards, wild areas, and much more. There is no reason why a large garden cannot provide a substantial part of what you eat every day of the year, with plenty to spare during high times.

The only limiting factor to what you can achieve in a large garden is the time you are able to dedicate to gardening, because there will be enough space to keep you occupied all the time if you so choose. Yet again—and I will keep emphasizing this point—a good plan is vital. Sketching on paper what you want to include will help focus your mind, allow you to cost items accurately, and enable you to think through a successful program of work. Your garden will only feel like a chore if simple but important functions are not well planned or if access to areas such as compost heaps is difficult. It is quite common, for example, to build a lovely area for sitting out, but one that misses the sun or requires access through areas that are soggy after rain, so putting you off using it and causing disappointment. Careful thought will always pay off and, while we all like to get stuck into a garden quickly, if you can bear to observe it for a season, then you'll make better plans. Don't regard this period of observation as a waste of time either, since you can spend that season preparing the ground with the BD 500

∧ There's no problem finding space for those all-important compost heaps in a large garden such as this.

> An orchard can provide fruit and a meadow habitat. It is also an ideal place for keeping bees, chickens, or even sheep.

biodynamic preparation, perhaps getting a compost heap going, or buying in a load of manure to rot down.

The discipline with which you then work in the early stages will determine whether your garden runs smoothly. If you take the time to set up heavily mulched, weed-free, no-dig beds, then you will only have to routinely hoe the surface. Thirty minutes of hoeing in the garden, when the weed seeds are just emerging, will save a whole day of weeding four weeks down the line. Saving time in this way allows you to concentrate on planting, raising seeds, or simply sitting back with a glass of wine and enjoying a summer evening.

Choosing your crops

As is the case with small- and medium-sized gardens, being clear from the start on what you want to achieve in your garden is of the utmost importance. Although a large space allows you to grow a wider selection of plants, it can be rewarding to grow different varieties of the same crop, as this can provide a range of colors and flavors, as well as picking and harvesting times. For example, you might decide to grow lots of tomato varieties, from cherry to plum, and from purple, through red, to yellow. Similarly, growing three different varieties of asparagus will give you a longer picking season, which can always seem so short in small spaces.

Large gardens not only provide plenty of space for a range of produce, but also for beneficial wildlife areas, which are so vital to a balanced, diverse ecosystem. By planning the site well, you will have everything covered and can enjoy life outdoors to the full.

∧ With plenty of space, there is room to try fun varieties like this black tomato, as well as traditional "doers."

∧   Essential hand tools include a hand fork, a planting trowel, hand pruners, a transplanting trowel, and a sharp knife.

A basic tool-kit

* ❋ SPADE
* ❋ FORK
* ❋ RAKE
* ❋ HOE
* ❋ GARDENING KNIFE
* ❋ HAND FORK
* ❋ HAND TROWEL
* ❋ HAND PRUNERS (SECATEURS)
* ❋ SEED TRAYS
* ❋ PLANT LABELS
* ❋ GARDEN SIEVE
* ❋ WATERING CAN
* ❋ WATER BUTT (FOR COLLECTING RAINWATER)
* ❋ BUCKET
* ❋ HORTICULTURAL FLEECE
* ❋ GARDEN CANES

Tools, Equipment, and Materials

If you are already gardening organically and simply wish to adhere to the cycles of the moon, as well as her relationship with the planets and stars, then you are already very well set up. The main item you will need, in addition to your current tool-kit, is a lunar calendar, several of which are available in different forms.

What do you need to get started?

If you are a non-organic gardener who wishes to adopt organic or biodynamic methods, then you may find yourself with some surplus equipment such as chemical sprayers. You will also discover that you use a fork far less and a hoe rather more frequently. You may, of course, find yourself in the wonderful position of being entirely new to gardening and without any equipment, so, not only are you faced with the excitement of growing, but you also have an opportunity to choose the perfect tools and equipment for you.

Everyone's approach to gardening is different, and over time you will probably find certain methods, tools, or materials that suit your physique, taste, and budget better. These preferences may change along the way and it's possible you will buy something that you don't ever use, so again some careful thought and planning is a good idea.

There is nothing like action, and getting stuck straight into a project, so, if you have made a good plan, then don't be afraid to get started. Of course, making sure you have certain tools such as a hoe, hand trowel, bucket, and watering can is important, although what you need will depend on the size of your growing space. Tools are also very personal, and I cover this in more detail in the next pages, but one simple rule is to purchase the best quality that your budget will allow. Some of my favorite tools can now be referred to as vintage and were purchased quite cheaply second-hand; on the other hand, there are also some very fine tools that I covet to this day, but have yet to justify buying.

Moon and biodynamic gardeners will also need an appropriate calendar, and it's worth keeping that close to hand. One of my calendars is on the wall next to the kitchen window, which is where I often stand and gaze out at the garden and sky.

If you are gardening biodynamically, then you will also need to buy the biodynamic preparations, primarily BD 500 and BD 501, at stages throughout the year. If you have a compost heap, you will have to purchase the relevant preparations for that, too. BD 500 and BD 501 need to be mixed in rainwater, so plan for this and have a mixing bucket to hand. (Be certain when collecting rainwater that it is not contaminated with chemicals, dirt, or atmospheric pollution. Water from glasshouse roofs is usually quite clean, but a storm after a dry spell can produce quite mucky water.) Making the transition to a fully biodynamic system will take several years and it all begins with the preparations, which start the soil-conditioning process. Garden compost is the second phase in repairing and improving the soil, but please remember that it takes a while to produce.

The following pages will help you select the best materials for successful maintenance, as well as plant rearing and growing, without wasting too many resources on unnecessary purchases.

Finding further help and advice

It is also well worth having good reference material to hand, whether in the form of a book or via the Internet. Nowadays, online searches are much better for finding advice, but you need to be sure of the sources and stick to websites you trust. I have found like-minded Facebook gardening groups really useful, plus there is a whole world of blogs and forums to explore. I have to say—and perhaps this is symptomatic of my generation—that it is hard to beat good old-fashioned books, though, and I have some on my shelf that have been reliable friends for many years.

∧ Essential gardening tools include a spade, hoe, soil rake, and garden fork.

< Labels are a must in the edible garden, helping you to keep track of what you are growing where.

Growing media for containers

Growing in pots and containers requires the use of certified organic growing media at the very least, which can then be improved with BD 500 or Mausdorf Starter (see page 78), as well as material from the compost heap if you have one. Standard multi-purpose potting media really aren't very good, having either been impregnated with fertilizer or needing additional artificial feeds to sustain the plants. Potting media are all too often simply something inert for the plants to take root in, but can have a poor nutrient content.

Seed

Seeds are pure energy and DNA, and the only way for a plant to ensure the future of its species. Just like humans, a good, healthy lifestyle increases the likelihood of strong reproduction and, as a plant cannot move to better ground, it relies upon the conditions in a very small space.

Commercial and biodynamic seed

Seed that has been raised commercially has probably been treated with chemicals, either in the form of fertilizer or to treat pests and diseases. Some commercial agricultural crops are even killed with herbicide just at the moment the seed is ripening to ensure that it all ripens at the same time—one can only wonder at what this does to the final quality. There will have been no adherence to the phases of the moon, which means that seed vigor and viability is a lottery, and that plants which grow from them will have the same genes only.

Biodynamic seed is produced and harvested in a very different way to commercial seed. In an established biodynamic garden, the seed will have been sown on the optimum day, in the optimum ground conditions, and the plant will continue to grow in this way. Insects will open-pollinate the flowers, ensuring genetic diversity, and the seed that is produced will only be collected at the optimum time. The energy and genetic material stored within that

∧   Successful gardening starts with good seed, so treat it well. You can prolong the life of seed by storing it in a wooden box.

>   Ripening in the summer sun, these poppy seedheads are concentrating their efforts on producing strong, healthy seed.

Collecting and storing seed

Collecting and storing seed is simple and rewarding. It isn't easy to collect seed from all plants, though, as some burst when ready and shower seed everywhere. However, plants like peas and beans are easy to collect from. Choose several favorite plants and watch to see which is the healthiest (don't collect from poor performers). Allow some of the crop to go to seed on your chosen plants. For example, on a runner bean plant, leave 10 pods to ripen and go brown. When the seed inside rattles, then the pod can be opened, dried a little further in a warm, dark place, and then stored in a paper envelope. For lettuce, leave one plant from a row to flower and set seed. Carefully watch the seed pods to work out when the seed is ready for collecting. As a rule, if the seeds inside are brown or black, then they are ready.

seed will have been highly attuned to the moon and will continue to deliver optimum results when it germinates. This is the continual cycle of life for plants, and only those that are propagated, raised, harvested, stored, and propagated again in the same disciplined way can be ultimately at their best. This can be seen very clearly in Nature where, when left alone, native flora soon takes hold of an opportunity with surprising skill and speed.

Sourcing and buying seed

There are various sources for buying biodynamic seed and, once you are up and running, you can harvest your own. However, not everybody will be able to do this, so what are your other options? The next best option is to source good organic seed from a reliable certified supplier, because it will have come from plants that are in a better, more natural state. If you search a little and find some good reviews, then you can easily determine the quality of the produce.

Should you find yourself in the situation of having to buy off-the-shelf, standard seed, then do not despair, as you can provide it with everything it needs from now on. Consider the purchase of this seed in the same way you would if taking on a rescue pet: improve its lifestyle and provide the care that it would always have liked.

In all cases it is important to use the freshest seed possible. While many seeds can be kept for several years, the conditions have to be just right, and it is easy to get this wrong and greatly reduce the viability. If you find yourself relying on older seed, then just factor in more than you need. Then, if you are lucky with strong germination, you have something to trade.

∧ Young beetroot seedlings huddle together in trays of small cells.

∧ Sown just before a full moon, and charged with energy, this two-day-old runner bean seedling stretches up to the sun.

through the sowing guidelines and separate the seed packets into months for sowing (although some seed will bridge months or have repeat sowings). As a biodynamic gardener, I then like to mark on the packets whether the seed is a flower, fruit, root, or leaf crop, so that everything is nicely organized and ready to go on the appropriate days.

With this all done, and working to a garden plan, you can begin the joyful time of sowing seed and raising lots of little offspring. Make sure at all times, however, that you store the seed in a dry, safe place, keeping the packets sealed and the conditions healthy.

Choosing what to grow

Sourcing seed is the first important stage, but knowing what to select when buying it is another critical factor. There are a great many seed varieties that grow well, producing the biggest, the longest, the shiniest, or the smelliest of something, but they are not necessarily what you want on your plate, in your garden, or in a vase. Often these champion plants do so well because of disease resistance or simple vigor, but do not taste that good when put to the test. A very good way to whittle this down is to follow the advice given by chefs or cooks that also garden and grow. There are also growers that supply good produce for the kitchens of fine restaurants and they, too, have a great knowledge of what chefs respond well to.

When buying seed, make a note of the packet's contents, and how far it will go, as you may end up with too few or too many. One runner bean seed, for example, will supply a lot of beans as a crop, and 10 bean plants a significant amount, whereas tiny carrot seeds soon get lost in a row and go even less far when thinned.

After placing your order, the exciting day comes when the seed arrives. This is a time I revel in. I really enjoy going through the neat little packets and checking what I have ordered—with a few surprises when I see that I've "ordered one of those as well." Firstly, you will need to run

Seed raised in biodynamic conditions will be strong, vibrant, and resistant to problems.

Organic Feeds and Tonics

When a problem occurs in the non-organic garden, we spray fungicide or pesticide, killing many living things, and then add a dose of feed for good measure. After that chemical battering, it's a wonder any plant is still growing and also little surprise that plants begin to rely on these treatments like any chemical-dependent life form. However, there are more natural ways to feed and nurture the soil and plants in your garden.

Homemade organic feeds and tonics have been used for a long time by gardeners. Not only are they free, but also very effective. Recent developments have meant that they are able to ferment more quickly—perhaps with more intense benefits—but the process is essentially unchanged. There are many recipes, often personal to the maker, all of which consist of steeping an ingredient or two in water to produce a liquid feed.

Making compost teas

Made from well-rotted garden compost, this tonic adds beneficial organisms to the soil, along with many of the trace nutrients that are required for healthy plant growth.

1. Half fill a bucket with mature garden compost. This ensures it has a sweet, earthy smell and not a bad odor.

2. Fill the bucket with water (rain or natural water is best) and allow to steep for at least a week. Stir the mix every day to incorporate oxygen on which bacteria can live. You'll find that the more the mix is stirred, the quicker it will work.

3. Strain the mix through a piece of muslin or similar, put the strainings back on the compost heap, and dilute the liquid with more water at a ratio of 50:50.

4. The resulting liquid should be used fresh by spraying or watering onto plants of all kinds, from hedge to vegetables.

Modern developments have taken this process further by adding food for the bacteria, for example, and using aquarium pumps to keep the water oxygenated. You can also buy various "brewing" kits online for making teas.

Making comfrey and nettle teas

Comfrey (*Symphytum* x *uplandicum*) or nettle (*Urtica dioica*) teas are very popular feeds in organic gardening. Using comfrey is particularly popular, as it harvests a wide range of nutrients from the soil and is also high in nitrogen. Other suitable plants are horsetail, bracken, clover, groundsel, and borage. To make an organic tea, follow these steps:

1. Gather a large bundle of leaves and/or fresh growing tips, and add them to a bucket or water tank.

2. Weigh the leaves down with a brick and fill the container with fresh water.

3. Stir the water and leaves, cover, and leave the rotting process to get underway. Some gardeners say that several days are enough, but more believe that several weeks are needed. The mix will begin to smell quite bad in a short time, but this is a sign that the process is working well. There should also be plenty of surface bubbles, which will be assisted by occasional stirring.

4. When you are happy with the result, strain the liquid, dilute it with water at a ratio of 1:10, and apply the feed to your plants.

Urine
Yes, as grotty as the idea may seem, collecting your urine, watering it down, and adding it to the garden is an excellent way to feed plants. Believe it or not, there will not be any issues with smell, as the watering down at a ratio of 1:20 dilutes it so much. What could be easier?

Cocktail mix
This is basically a mix of just about anything you have available, but ideally might include comfrey, nettle, a shovel of well-rotted manure, weeds, or even urine. Add the ingredients to a large water barrel with a tap for drawing off the liquid and leave to brew for several weeks. In much the same way, draw off the resulting feed, dilute with water at a ratio of 1:10, and water onto the whole garden. The wonderful results will be noticeable.

Collecting nettle stems for nettle tea. Young stems, without flowers, are a better choice.

∨ After three days, the nettles begin to break down, releasing their precious stored nutrients.

Biodynamic Preparations

If you are making the transition from being an organic to a biodynamic gardener, then you will need to use the biodynamic preparations. There are eight preparations, which are applied in one of two ways: BD 500 and BD 501 are watered onto the soil or plants, while the remaining six are added to the compost heap.

Preparations for watering onto the soil and plants

BD 500 or Horn Dung Preparation is applied to the soil to promote germination, moisture levity, microorganism growth, and root growth, and acts upon the very foundations of the soil. It is the first treatment to apply, both to a new biodynamic garden and also each growing season, and prepares the soil for subsequent preparations. It is made by packing pure cow dung into a cow's horn, burying it to overwinter, break down, and become a powdered ingredient for watering onto the garden.

BD 501 or Horn Quartz Preparation is sprayed onto plants to stimulate photosynthesis and the formation of chlorophyll. It helps with the ripening stage during a plant's lifecycle, and is applied to crops that are well under way, perhaps a month before fruiting. It is made from finely ground quartz crystal, which is added to rainwater to make a paste, and again buried in a cow's horn, but this time over the summer. The resulting powder is again mixed with water and sprayed in a fine mist onto plants.

Preparations for adding to the compost heap

The following preparations are added to the compost heap and assist in the production of perfect potentized garden compost. Each one is prepared in a different way: some are stuffed into animal intestines or bladders, while others are simply buried before being harvested and prepared for use.

∨ Cow horn preparations exhumed and ready for use after a season of burial.

∨ A single unit of Horn Dung Preparation or BD 500, as purchased online.

∨ A single unit of Horn Silica Preparation or BD 501, as purchased online.

YARROW BLOSSOM
(*Achillea millefolium*) PREP 502
Yarrow is connected with the processes of sulfur and potassium, and the uptake of these trace elements. The blossoms are stuffed into the bladder of a deer and then hung in the sunlight of summer. In the fall (autumn), the bladder is buried for the winter and then dug up the following summer after a full year. By this stage the yarrow will have been "charged" by Earth and planetary forces, and be highly potent to plants.

CHAMOMILE BLOSSOM
(*Matricaria chamomilla*) PREP 503
The chamomile preparation helps to stabilize nitrogen in the soil, stimulates microorganisms, and therefore aids plant growth. The blossoms are stuffed into the small intestine of a cow and then twisted into little sausages before being buried to overwinter. These are then dug up at around Easter for use.

STINGING NETTLE
(*Urtica dioica*) PREP 504
The nettle vitalizes and enlivens the soil, being rich in iron and silica. Nettles are cut when in flower and quite simply buried in fertile soil for a year.

OAK BARK
(*Quercus robur or Q. alba*)
PREP 505
The oak bark preparation helps to neutralize alkaline soils without the need for adding lime, encouraging healthy calcium processes. It is a "healing" addition, regulating calcium, lush growth and flushes of fungal disease. Fresh bark is gathered from living trees, powdered, and stuffed into the skull of a cow, sheep, or goat. It is buried to overwinter in moist ground and dug up the following spring.

DANDELION BLOSSOM
(*Taraxacum officinale*)
PREP 506
This is another preparation that is connected with silica. The blossoms are stuffed into a cow's mesentery, which is the layer that surrounds the intestines, and buried in the ground from fall (autumn) until spring.

VALERIAN BLOSSOM
(*Valeriana officinalis*) PREP 507
This preparation helps plant roots access phosphorus in the soil. It is made from the juice of valerian flowers and applied to the outside of the compost heap.

(For further advice on preparing and using these biodynamic preparations, see *Mixing and Using Biodynamic Treatments, pages 74–5, and The Biodynamic Compost Heap, pages 76–9.*)

A Country Garden

Kate's garden in Kent, UK, is medium-sized with an area of ⅓ acre (0.1 hectares). The large lawn is lined with cobnut and fruit trees. The vegetable garden is approximately 323 square feet (30 square meters), and there's a glasshouse. The soil is fairly sandy with some clay content, which makes it free draining. It has a pH of around 7.0.

Kate Wrigglesworth has gardened for as long as she can remember, and has always enjoyed both ornamental and vegetable gardening. Following a career in chemistry, she is very aware of the effects that chemicals can have and so has always made an effort to garden and eat organically. Until recently she was a devoted digger. However, the death of her father led to a season when she had less time to spend in the garden. At this time she also heard of the no-dig approach, which she then employed out of both interest and necessity. Kate is so pleased with the results that she is planning to continue in this way because, as she says, "After all, it gets rid of the back-breaking work, and grows good produce."

This year Kate began following the lunar calendar at my suggestion. She has followed sowing and planting days accurately, as well as

Kate has a large garden, but her vegetable beds are relatively compact, making them easy to manage whilst providing well for two.

Tomatoes fresh from the garden taste so much better, are chemical free and have not had their flavor damaged by refrigeration.

∧ Basking in sunlight, Kate's no dig beds grow productive, healthy plants.

> Onions dry in the sun, next to the added shelter of the orchard trees.

watering by the moon, and has tried where possible to tend plants on the correct elemental days. So far this year, she has also harvested at the right time, and will continue to do so with her tree fruit in the fall (autumn). She has been guided by Nick Kollerstrom's moon gardening calendar, and has found it easy to follow, as well as practical. Being retired, Kate has been able to plan her time around the garden and keep quite strictly to the optimum times.

Her influences have trickled in from all over, as is often the way with widely read gardeners. She highlights Geoff Hamilton as a gardener who stood out and from whom she has taken direct inspiration. Her no-dig direction stemmed from reading a review of a Charles Dowding publication by Maddy Harland who is an expert on permaculture. So, is she pleased with the results? Absolutely, and she plans to continue with both not digging and moon gardening next year.

"Gardening keeps me grounded. I also like to know where my food comes from, to have it fresh and chemical-free. From the garden it simply tastes so much better too."

Soil and Compost:
The Foundations of it All

All land-dwelling life relies on soil to exist. Soil
gives us the building blocks for nourishment, as
well as the minerals to grow and develop, and it
is to the soil that all life returns upon death.
This unbreakable cycle would not work without
the process of composting, which turns
past life into food and energy again,
only to be recycled by the next generation
of living organisms. It's not hard to see why this
subject is so very important, for without soil and
composting there would be no gardening, no
agriculture, and no life. Giving your garden the
perfect foundations of good soil and compost
will allow you to build a remarkable masterpiece
that can withstand difficult times, while also
providing sumptuous pleasure.

All About Soil

Soil, earth, dirt, mud—there are many words to describe the uppermost layer of our planet. As well as being the material on which we walk, soil is also an essential source of life. It comes in many forms, can be very localized, and therefore has a huge influence on what plant life can grow, the cultures and traditions of indigenous peoples, and the subsequent industries of the developing world. For millennia, mankind worked with the soil in a symbiotic relationship of sustainable living, while in recent centuries we have developed ever more powerful ways of adapting the soil to our advantage.

It is little wonder then that this "giver of life" should be such an incredibly complex subject. In fact, if I were to devote the book to soil alone, it would still only scratch the surface of this fascinating subject. A handful of soil can contain millions of organisms and a widely varied sample of minerals and gases, making it the most genetically diverse environment on Earth. As the "surface" of the Earth, it is also the receiver of everything that reaches the ground from above, be this water-based, air (composed of various gases), or radiated energy from the sun and moon.

As gardeners, soil is our most precious resource and so should be the main focus of our attentions. If we put enough effort into nurturing and caring for our soil, it will reward us with bountiful crops and jaw-dropping displays. Despite the complexity of soil, we don't need to be soil scientists to understand it, interpret what it requires from us, or to work with it when making our gardens.

Soil structure

You will often hear gardeners talk about soil structure. This refers to the very specific make-up of the soil in a particular area or even in your own garden. The structure of the soil in an area is affected by many factors, including history of cultivation, activities on the soil surface, climate, and chemical intervention, but it is generally based on a mixture of key ingredients. These ingredients are largely composed of the particles laid down by geological activity in the area, as well as long-term land characteristics. The local natural stone will also have a bearing, as will the course or location of ancient rivers, seabeds, and forests, or perhaps the more recent activity of rivers, estuaries, or flood plains.

Soil is made up of various minerals, organic matter, gases, water, and living organisms. The mixture of these elements will vary, so giving rise to different types of soil, such as sandy, silty or clay (see page 67). The type of soil will usually be typical over a wide area, making gardening and agriculture in such areas follow certain themes.

∧ Vibrant and full of promise, these young zucchini (courgette) plants are thriving as a result of great soil.

Soil mulched with plenty of organic matter builds the perfect soil structure for stable, strong and healthy plant growth.

Soil type can, of course, be altered through cultivation, but this is not always a wise course to follow, often leading to significant physical, mental, and financial effort.

The best environment for plant growth is a soil made up of 50% solids (that is, 45% mineral solids and 5% organic matter) and 50% voids, which contain either air (made up of various gases) or water. The ratio of solids to voids varies continually, being influenced by habitat, weather, and season. Soil compaction is a major contributor to poor growing conditions because it reduces the volume of voids, so allowing in less air and water, which are key components of living soil.

The most important components of soil are clay and humus particles. Their role is to store nutrients that might otherwise leach away. Put simply, nutrients come in mineral form and are released to plants by the activity of soil microorganisms, with the exception of nitrogen, which is produced by bacteria. Organic matter has a similar importance, since it can also retain moisture and nutrients for plants to access. It also provides an active habitat for soil organisms, both tiny and large.

However, the most important factor regarding the availability of nutrients to plants is soil pH, which in extremes can render nutrients entirely unavailable. Generally speaking, soil pH is acceptable for a range of plants in most areas of human habitation, but some plant groups may be excluded at either end of the safe growing spectrum. Most plants perform well at pH 5.5 to 6.5, an acidic soil in which minerals and nutrients are easily dissolved and so readily available to plants. Many plants will tolerate a pH as high as 9.0—which is an alkaline soil—but the availability of nutrients becomes problematic beyond this point.

∧ My garden is on deep, heavy clay, which many gardeners dread. With a thick layer of dark, almost black, organic matter, the soil structure is perfect for growing.

Soil in the garden

When left alone soil develops a natural, balanced structure which, if cut through cleanly, is usually made up of layers. The surface is generally covered with a thin skim of organic matter, and is dependent on the plant life that creates it. Below that is a layer of topsoil. This layer may be shallow or deep, and is where much of the life and activity goes on—the party zone, if you like. Next is a layer of sub-soil, which might be stony, dense clay, or perhaps chalk, but with less life and only thicker, structural root activity. Finally, there is the bedrock, which is commonly the source of the main solid mineral ingredient. Of course, all this can vary depending on the area, where there may be little or no topsoil, or organic matter, and then bedrock.

As gardeners we aim to develop a good, healthy soil structure, which provides the perfect growing environment for a wide range of plants. This structure is critical to our long-term growing efforts and, as I have mentioned before, is the most precious thing we have. Modern farming techniques have greatly influenced gardening, meaning that significant soil intervention is now normal practice. Perfect soil is an incredibly delicate balance, and a very natural one at that. Every mechanical operation—and by this I include humans digging—that is undertaken disturbs this balance, causing seismic change to a microscopic world. The addition of any inorganic, unnatural substance such as fertilizer or herbicide further degrades that balance, and begins a sequence of ever-increasing degradation of the environment in which organisms can create natural nutrients. It is in healthy, well-balanced soil that you will find the root of Rudolf Steiner's theories and the path to successful growing.

Your soil

So, what does this mean practically in your own garden? Understanding your soil is important, so, if you haven't already, you'll need to find out about it. Talk to neighbors (though remember always to apply a reality filter here) and have a look at other gardens, but most of all get out there and look. Dig a hole in several places and see how the soil is made up. Look at how deep your topsoil is and whether it is stony. Get a small fist of moist soil and try rolling it into a ball. If it keeps crumbling, then your soil is sandy; if it almost sticks, but loosely, then it is silty; and if it makes a lovely, smooth, solid ball, then it is clay. (For more on different soil types and methods of improving them, see page 67.)

Looking into the hole you will also be able to see what layers you have, whether or not there is a decent layer of organic matter (this is usually darker in color at the surface), and if there are plenty of grubs and creepy crawlies. Beyond this you might like to get a soil-testing kit to work out the soil pH, for example, or perhaps send a sample away to be analyzed.

Improving and caring for this wonderful, life-giving organism is covered in detail throughout the following pages of this chapter. However, I cannot stress heavily enough that good soil is the key to healthy plants, a healthy patch of your planet, and a wholesome existence. There really is no need to bash it about every year, to mix up the layers, to break the 50:50 balance of solids and voids, to add nasty, man-made substances, and to ruin that lovely environment for beneficial organisms. Treat your soil well and it will give you everything you need in return.

Taking time to create the best soil conditions for plant health and vitality is just as important in the ornamental garden.

Gardening Without Digging

Whether for vegetables or ornamental displays, gardening need not involve digging. For several hundred years it has been traditional to turn the soil over and add organic matter as deeply as possible. It was not always thus, however, and a routine light cultivation of a well-prepared surface is perfectly sufficient for establishing healthy plants. This is a personal preference, proven over decades, but still only practiced by a minority because, for some reason, we like to see well-dug soil in spite of the back-breaking effort required. There are a number of biodynamic farms that cultivate heavily and have good results, but it's my preference for not digging that I shall emphasize in this book.

No-dig gardening, as it is commonly called, concentrates on leaving the delicately balanced, layered structure of the soil undisturbed. Every season organic matter is added to the surface of the soil in thin mulches, which in time creates a light, slightly raised, and nutrient-rich top layer. Activity from soil organisms breaks it down, while at the same time aerating and improving the structure below. Narrow beds avoid any soil compaction, allowing the ratio of air and water to be just right, and are also a good size for easy maintenance. It is a method that suits all soil types, is particularly effective on clay soils, and can transform even a lawn into vegetable beds in months.

Creating a no-dig garden

Starting entirely from scratch, or converting your existing garden to a system free of digging, is very simple. It is not without labor, but this labor is exceedingly useful and ten times more rewarding. The stages opposite show what's involved in turning an area of lawn into vegetable beds. I made this garden in the spring after moving to a new house, and was rewarded with a summer of growing leaf crops.

Layout

In my garden, I mulched and covered the entire vegetable plot, which I then made into 3ft (1m) wide beds running from front to back. These narrow beds are easy to work, weed, and harvest without standing on them and so compacting the soil. Between each bed is a narrow path that is simply mulched in the same way, but compacted by foot. You may only choose to mulch the beds, which will work just as well. This means you can have grass, paved, or soft-covered paths (that is, bark or gravel), thus allowing access while the no-dig conversion is taking place.

< Charles Dowding's narrow, no-dig vegetable beds are perfect for creating the right soil structure, as well as for garden maintenance with maximum efficiency.

Preparing beds for planting

(1) Sourcing mulch
The key to this is good, rich organic matter, which in this first application needs to be deep (4–6in/10–15cm). I tracked down some cow manure, which was a year old, although older is better. Any well-rotted manure will do or, if you have a good quantity of composted garden waste, then that is also excellent. The area featured is 16 x 10ft (5 x 3m) and I applied about 70 cubic feet (2 cubic metres) of manure.

(2) Adding a cardboard layer
Once you have sourced the mulch, you need to find enough cardboard boxes to flatten over the area. The idea is to prevent any light reaching the lawn or weeds below, and to provide a physical barrier against those that still have a go. Remove any tape first and be sure to overlap the cardboard so that plants have no route out. By the time the weeds and grass have spent their energy and died, the cardboard will have broken down to almost nothing.

(3) Applying a mulch
Adding a layer of mulch serves multiple purposes, but initially it will hold the cardboard in place. When spreading the mulch, be sure not to displace the boxes and create gaps. Time spent doing this right will pay off. Systematically working across the area, add a nice deep layer of your chosen mulch to a depth of 4–6in (10–15cm), which will further add to the physical and optical barrier of the cardboard.

(4) Covering the area
You now need to cover the area and wait. The best option is to lay black polythene over the entire area and weight it down against wind. Over a period of at least two months the unwanted plants will die and soil organisms, including worms, will chomp through the mulch of organic matter. They will break it down and start blending it with the soil below, creating the beginning of a fine surface tilth for sowing and planting.

(5) Removing the plastic
It is hard to say when is the best time to remove the plastic covering, as this depends on when you started. This is a good fall (autumn) project, since it leaves the winter for the mulch to break down, but you will need to wait a little while into spring so any dormant plants that try to germinate are killed. Wait at least one month after everything around you has got going and then all should be well. If you do this during spring or summer, then the plants under the mulch will be killed off quickly, but the mulch will still need a little time to break down. Give it a minimum of two months if the mulch is good and longer if it is quite fresh. The manure used for this project was a little too fresh and I had to start growing before it was perfect, but no weeds came through and the young plants thrived.

Maintaining Healthy Soil

Creating good, well-laid-out, organically rich beds is one thing, but keeping them in good shape is another. While the first step is the hardest physically, keeping your soil in a balanced and harmonious state takes thought, planning, and some skill. Reassuringly, however, it is a simple process to follow and easily achieved if you pay attention, notice how your plants are performing, and keep in touch with ever-present Nature.

I have already mentioned that there is no need to dig. This task will all be taken care of by worms and other organisms, winter freezing and thawing, rain, root activity, summer hoeing, and harvesting. These processes are far better for developing the right soil structure than our mechanical and intrusive methods. Our efforts are best focused on keeping the garden free of competitive weeds and, most of all, not letting weeds go to seed, as well as feeding and dressing the surface of the soil.

Hoeing off weeds

Using a hoe to control weeds is by far the most effective and certainly the quickest method if it is done at the right time. Weed seedlings die quickly if they are hoed at the time of germination, or at no more than a week old, which also means they have no chance at all of setting seed. Once you have your garden under control, a very large area can be hoed in half an hour, which would take all day if left to become a fork, hands, and knees job. A quick weekly round with the hoe will not only keep weeds in check, but also over time depreciate the weed-seed bank in the soil, which will result in far fewer seeds germinating.

> Hoeing off small weeds between rows of vegetables quickly controls weeds at an early stage.

Useful tip

Limited interference with the soil allows the structure to balance itself well, while continually being fed and improved from the surface. In this way, all soil becomes a wonderfully bio-diverse environment that will provide healthy growing conditions for your plants.

Applying garden compost

Maintaining a nutritious soil ensures plants grow healthily, with great flowers and taste, and with such zest that they are less susceptible to pest and disease problems. This is achieved by adding a light dressing of garden compost or very well-rotted manure to the surface of the beds as often as possible. If you are growing vegetables, you should add a dressing each time a section is harvested or cleared, ready for the next crop to go in. For ornamental borders, add the dressing in winter following a tidy-up. A dressing of just an inch is sufficient when adding organic matter to a healthy soil, just as long as this is a routine operation.

In the biodynamic garden the compost dressing can be even lighter, since you are using compost made in a biodynamic heap (see pages 76–9). You will also be adding the soil preparation BD 500 twice a year, which conditions the soil even more.

∨ This commercially produced garden compost, the result of domestic garden refuse composted in huge heaps, is about two months old.

Working with different soil types

Soil is composed of three main particle types: sand, silt, and clay. The percentage of each of these particles determines how the soil behaves, and there are various descriptive soil categories, including sandy, sandy loam, loam, clay silt, and so on. Loam is about the most balanced, having equal measures of each particle type, but it is not common, so we must work with what we have.

CLAY
Characteristics: Dense, does not drain well, is prone to compaction, does not easily weather away, is nutrient-rich and capable of holding high additional levels of nutrients, remains moist for the longest during drought.
How to improve: Due to its moisture retention and high nutrient levels, clay is, in fact, a very desirable soil to grow in. Problems with excessive wet and compaction are easily overcome using the no-dig method of only dressing the surface (see pages 18 and 64), as well as by working narrow beds with access paths (see page 64). In time the narrow beds become slightly raised and drain well, while having a light and fluffy tilth at the surface that is high in organic matter. It

becomes easy to plant plugs or to sow directly, and the roots can then tap into the moist, nutrient-rich clay below.

SAND
Characteristics: Lighter, free-draining, not prone to compaction, can easily wash or blow away, does not hold nutrients easily, dries quickly during drought.
How to improve: Sandy soil needs lots of organic matter to aid the retention of moisture and nutrients. The activity of a myriad organisms produces humus, which has the ability to hold nutrients and moisture. A no-dig system (see pages 18 and 64) keeps this nutritious layer closer to the surface in sandy soils, which means that it is closer to the plants' roots. If you apply a good thick layer of organic matter, then this will keep the soil moist for longer.

SILT
Characteristics: Somewhere between clay and sand, but still not great at storing nutrients.
How to improve: Silty soils benefit from limited disturbance, as do other soil types.

Compost Explained

The term compost is a cause of much confusion. In the United Kingdom, for example, you can buy potting compost in bags from a garden center, while at the same time have compost heaps in the garden that produce an entirely different substance. To further add to the confusion you can now find recycled green wastes, manures, and all forms of organic matter available in bags under the bracket of "compost."

In the horticultural trade we differentiate between potting media (which is often called potting compost or potting mix) and garden compost. Potting media are the substances produced for growing plants in pots and containers, often being a blend of organic and mineral materials, and sometimes containing artificial feeds and pesticides. This is the same product that can be purchased from garden centers. It might contain loam, peat, recycled waste, coir, sylva fiber, and other materials, usually contains added fertilizer (unless it is certified organic), and is blended for either multi-purpose use or specific plant types.

Garden compost is the material that results from the natural process of composting, which goes on in various forms in garden compost heaps. It is made up of a variety of ingredients, which depend on the owner of the heap, all of which break down due to the activity of a range of organisms, resulting in a dark brown, crumbling material made of well-rotted organic matter.

We use other substances in horticulture to improve the soil. These are sometimes called mulch or organic matter and include various animal manures, bark/wood chips, community green wastes, mushroom compost, hop waste, and so on… While these need to rot or compost as well, they are made up of one or two ingredients. For this reason, they do not qualify as compost and have specific characteristics.

< A wide range of ingredients makes for good compost. Here, my heap contains lots of kitchen scraps, as well as old potting compost, weeds, chicken bedding, and lawn mowings.

∧ One new and one old;
when fully filled the
compost heap on the left
will break down and be
useable, like the one on
the right, within a year.

> These large, homemade
compost bins have good
volume and airflow, so
will heat up, and break
down quickly.

What makes good compost?

Good compost is easy to make, free, and a bi-product of normal life. There are some simple rules for what can be added to a compost heap, but you can generally pick and choose from anything you have available. Firstly, if the ingredient originated from a plant, then it can be composted, whether cooked or not. This includes weeds, lawn clippings, soft prunings and trimmings, as well as kitchen wastes like salad, vegetables, bread crusts, pasta, rice, and much more. I also add meat waste, although I waste little of this, so fish skins, small bones, and general leftovers.

The manure from herbivores is another good addition, from small pets as well as large ones, and I also add chicken muck and bedding when cleaning them out. I always instinctively avoid dog and cat waste, along with that of any other carnivore, even if the animal is on a vegetarian diet. Urine is very beneficial to the composting process, so if I need to go when in the garden, then the compost heap gets a treat. Biodynamic compost heaps are slightly different, and dealt with separately on pages 76–79.

Knowing what ingredients can be used is important, but, like any good cake, the quantities also have to be right. There needs to be a good balance of "woody" and green waste to keep the heap healthy. Too much straw, for example, leaves the heap dry and slow to compost, whereas too many lush grass clippings will result in a slimy, anaerobic mess. In my garden, I add bedding from the chicken house, weeds from the garden, leaves, and lawn mowings. I also add all the household waste mentioned above, followed by the dead top-growth of perennials when I'm clearing beds. From time to time I add some manure if I have it, which is a nice way to keep the heap lively. When the heap is full I cover the top with a plastic sheet and start a new one.

You need to make sure that the moisture level of the compost heap is correct. It's

∨ Compost heaps should be well positioned for practical access, but perhaps screened by some pretty planting. If carefully made, they can be attractive in their own right.

V A full compost heap with the front removed, showing the many layers of balanced ingredients.

∧ Squash plants grow well on compost heaps, benefitting from the heat of decomposition. In turn, their root activity works to break down the compost further.

very hard to say what is right: too dry and activity will stop; too wet and the heap will be suffocated and stop working. In most seasons, rain will keep the heap moist enough, but you will have to water your heap in dry spells, little and often being the best way. To ascertain if a heap is working well, you only need dig in a little way. If moist decomposition is racing along (the heap is often so hot that it creates steam), then you know all is well. Large, well-balanced heaps tend to stay sufficiently moist due to the fast, vigorous action of the composting process.

A hot, active heap will compost most things, but it is worth taking great care when adding perennial weeds or weeds that have already gone to seed. The roots of perennial thugs such as bindweed (*Calystegia sepium* or *Convolvulus arvensis*), couch grass (*Elymus repens*), and dandelions (*Taraxacum officinale*) are best thrown away or put on a separate long-term compost heap (putting only the top growth on the heap). The seed on weeds that are pulled just too late may survive the composting process, so again be cautious of this.

Building a Compost Heap

There are many ways in which to compost organic matter, from a simple pile in a corner of the garden to fancy hot-boxes and compost accelerators. Composting is an entirely natural process, which is in no need of technological interference, and quite quickly produces a very useable material.

∨ A standard plastic home composting bin. This is a good size and also neat and tidy for small gardens. I have made excellent garden compost in bins such as this.

I have personally used several options for containing my compost heap, the easiest being a plastic composting bin. Open at the bottom and wider too, with a lid on the top, I have found these simple compost bins work very well indeed. Within one year a full bin produces compost that can be sieved a little to make good potting media or spread directly onto beds. The largest heap I have worked has been a commercial "windrow," 20ft (6m) long and 6ft (1.8m) high. Turned with a tractor three times, these heaps get very hot and kill off even the worst perennial weeds, but are only suitable for large gardens.

My favorite structure for a compost heap is one made from reclaimed transport pallets because the heap will be easy to make, a good size, breathe freely, and give good access when removing the compost. To build one of these, you will need to obtain four matching pallets—I found mine at a local builders' merchant.

Composting tips

✳ The heap will do best if it is in contact with soil and this is essential for a biodynamic heap. If the heap is sitting on a hard surface, then dark brown juices will ooze out and can stain the area, as well as being pungent.

✳ People worry that compost heaps will attract rats and other rodents. Both part of Nature, I don't mind them being about and, yes, they have visited my compost heaps, but never been a problem. The worst I have had is crows stealing perfectly good waste from the top of the heap and this was easily solved by covering it. Some plastic options have a mesh base to prevent rodents getting in, but you can also avoid the problem by not adding any food waste to your heap.

✳ A compost heap can have a mild odor, so be thoughtful as to where you position it.

How to build a compost bin

(1) **Selecting the pallets**
There are many pallet variations, so try to find pallets that are strong, but which you can lift. Avoid those with a solid base or wide gaps. You are looking for pallets with evenly spaced gaps of a similar width to the wooden slats. If you can get four matching ones, then even better.

(2) **Attaching the netting**
This is not entirely necessary, but many items on the heap will be quite small, so it is a good idea to line the pallets with narrow gauge chicken or rabbit wire. Using a 25mm or 1-inch grade wire will retain most materials, while allowing the heap to "breathe" freely. Staple the wire to each pallet independently so that it can be deconstructed and moved in the future.

(3) **Constructing the bin**
On a level surface, and ensuring the heap will be in contact with the soil, place two pallets together and join the corners top and bottom with strong galvanized wire. Repeat the process with the following two pallets to create a rigid square structure. An alternative is to hammer two stakes through each pallet to hold them up, which is a more permanent option. I like the wire because I can then move the pallets about easily.

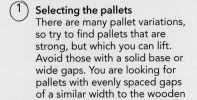

(4) **Adding the materials**
Once the bin is finished, you can start adding materials to the heap, following the advice given on page 77.

(5) **The composting process**
The materials will quickly begin to decompose and, with the right ingredients, the heap is likely to generate quite a temperature. You can kick-start the process by putting a little old compost or a nice bit of active manure in the bottom. I have two heaps in my garden (shown here), so that one can sit and decompose once full, while I start adding material to the other.

(6) **Using the compost**
The material is ready when it has become fine and crumbly throughout most of the heap. It can now be added directly onto the garden or sieved for use in containers. There may be a layer at the top that is not quite ready, but this can be taken off and put on the current heap.

Mixing and Using Biodynamic Treatments

The two biodynamic treatments or "preparations" that are most frequently used in the garden are BD 500 and BD 501 (horn manure and horn silica, respectively). Rather like homeopathic medicines, the ingredients are mixed in a very specific way to energize the preparation, which results in a beneficial change. You will be familiar with other mixtures that change with agitation, including omelets, cakes, bread, sauces, and building products, for example, so it is little wonder that agitation has a similar effect on biodynamic treatments as well.

Mixing the treatments

The aim with biodynamic preparations is to agitate the mixture with rhythm and chaos, introducing a large surface area of oxygen and giving time for radiated energy from the cosmos to have an influence. It is interesting to note that a fast-flowing, splashing, gushing mountain stream feels much more vibrant than a slow, easy river. It glistens with light, cools but enlivens the spirit, and is deeply refreshing—and it, too, experiences chaotic disturbance.

During the mixing process a portion of the main ingredient is added to clean water, which is contained in a suitable vessel (one made from a natural material is best but, failing that, a plastic bucket will do). You then need to get comfortable, as the agitation process can take up to an hour, so choose a nice spot. Select a wooden stirring tool, or use your hand and arm, and begin stirring the water vigorously until a vortex is created in the center. When the vortex is deep, stop stirring and wait a few seconds before stirring in the same way, but in the opposite direction. Once again, create a deep vortex and stop, before again reversing the stir. This systematic process is carried out until the very consistency of the water changes, which you will be able to sense with experience, but at the outset should happen within an hour.

It is also important to be mindful of what you are doing, and to try and focus your thoughts on the procedure. You are aiming to connect with every layer of the garden and to get involved at a fundamental level, so let yourself be absorbed in the process. In this way, you are more likely to sense changes in the mixture and to "feel" when it is ready.

Applying BD 501 as a fine mist to the garden, in a sprayer suitable to the smallest of spaces

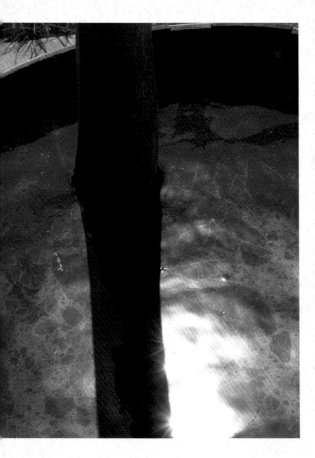

∧ At Tablehurst Farm the preparations are mixed in large wooden barrels, in volumes suitable for use on fields.

> Mixing the preparations is a special moment, being a chance to reflect, concentrate, and bring mindfulness to the process.

Using the treatments

It is important to use the preparations quickly, so be prepared for this before you start. BD 500 needs to be sploshed or flicked about in large droplets, so get a clean, coarse brush or bundle of twigs and flick the preparation as you walk about the garden. This is best done in the afternoon, when the mixture is drawn down into the soil most effectively. BD 501 must be applied in a fine mist, so use a clean spray bottle that has not been contaminated with any chemicals and spray directly onto leaves in the morning, when the preparation can be taken up into the plant.

As a soil treatment, BD 500 can be applied at various times and to suit your feelings. Early spring, early summer, and fall (autumn) are all good key stages. Some gardeners like to treat the soil more frequently or each time they plant. BD 501 is for healthy growth, as well as fruit/flower production and ripening, so is best applied during the growing season. On large crops it can be applied very specifically prior to ripening, but can be used more generally in small gardens.

The Biodynamic Compost Heap

A biodynamic compost heap is not dissimilar to a traditional organic compost heap in its ingredients or the way in which a balanced, layered heap is built up, but it has the added benefit of biodynamic "rocket fuel." In a large, high-production biodynamic garden or farm the compost heaps are made in one go, using all the required ingredients, but this is not practical in a domestic garden. For this reason I shall concentrate on smaller compost heaps that are added to little and often, which is what you are most likely to have.

Having several compost heaps allows for a more continuous supply. Here, the mature heap (left) is being used, while the one on the right has recently been filled to the brim.

A biodynamic compost heap features the addition of several herbal treatments, a little soil, and, if possible, cow manure. The herbal treatments were highlighted by Rudolph Steiner as playing a key role in healing and improving soil, each being used for ancient medicinal treatments as well. These are:

Prep 502 (Yarrow blossom/*Achillea millefolium*),
Prep 503 (Chamomile blossom/*Matricaria chamomilla*),
Prep 504 (Stinging nettle/*Urtica dioica*),
Prep 505 (Oak bark/*Quercus robur* or *Q. alba*),
Prep 506 (Dandelion blossom/*Taraxacum officinale*), and
Prep 507 (Valerian blossoms/*Valeriana officinalis*).

While these biodynamic treatments can be made at home, it is easiest and best to purchase them from a biodynamic association that operates on a small scale. (See *Biodynamic Preparations*, pages 54–5, for more information on the different preparations.)

Cow manure is essential to the well-balanced workings of a biodynamic farm, ensuring that it can exist as a single organism. Cows have a highly developed digestive system which transforms their food so cleanly into the best feed for plants that it is a highly valued ingredient for the compost heap. Few of us have space for a cow, but it is often possible to get hold of cow manure from a local farmer. Manure from an organic farm is best but, if you cannot find this, any other manure will do, but be cautious of farms that spray selective herbicides onto their pastures and fodder crops. Some herbicides, such as Aminopyralid, can pass through the digestive system of animals and remain in their manure for some time, which I suspect has happened to me in the past and I know to have happened to others. These herbicides greatly reduce the growth of a range of plants and poison soil. If cow manure is unavailable, then other herbivore manures will do, but be equally aware of the source and quality of the animals' original feed.

Preparations and the planets

Some biodynamic gardeners, but not all, believe the plants used in the preparations are associated with the planets in our solar system, further linking the energies of the cosmos to the soil. As with the theory that the moon passing in front of constellations has a specific effect on plants, this identifies another link between plants and the cosmos. Therefore, yarrow is linked to Venus, chamomile to Mercury, nettle to Mars, dandelion to Jupiter, and valerian to Saturn and Mars.

Adding a little soil from time to time has the benefit of introducing beneficial organisms to the composting process. I also find that the soil helps to make the compost more "loamy," or a little more dense, and therefore good as a potting compost.

When to add the ingredients?

In the case of small garden compost heaps, or even if you have a large garden, the heap is most practically added to periodically (or daily in my case). When starting from scratch, it is good to have something to give the heap a little body, which may be some lawn clippings, the results of an hour or so of weeding, or the cleaning out of a pet house. If you have an old heap that is ready to use, then the top of it skimmed off is perfect for this. As soon as you are under way, then a thin sprinkle of good soil can be added, a little more waste, and then a little manure. Continue like this until the heap container is about half full (don't be shocked if you think you've got to that stage and only a day or so later it has sunk by 50%, as composting works fast). At this stage the biodynamic treatments can be added by rolling each into a ball and dropping them into individually made holes toward the center of the heap. The exception to the rule is that Prep 507 is added in a solution to the outside of the heap once complete. Having done this, you can continue adding layers of ingredients to the heap until it is full. At this point, leave the heap to get on with its magical work before returning to use it when all is ready.

Other compost treatments

It is not always possible to get hold of the six biodynamic compost preparations and finding manure is problematic for many people, too. Fortunately, two alternatives have been developed that achieve a similar, if not quite as potent, effect. Ehrenfried Pfeiffer was a student of Steiner, a skilled biodynamic practitioner, and a microbiologist. He recognized that not everyone could make a compost heap as developed by Steiner, and set about finding an alternative. The result is the Pfeiffer Compost Starter, which adds the ideal range of organisms and trace elements of the compost preps directly to the heap. If you use this starter, then you don't even need manure, making it ideal for small heaps and gardens in urban areas.

The second alternative is the Barrel Compost developed by Maria Thun. This is also a way of adding traces of each herbal treatment, and is made by mixing cow muck (without straw) with eggshells and basalt. Once stirred, Preps 500, 501, and 507 are added and the whole mix buried for several months. The resulting "compost" is then energized in water, as with Preps 500 and 501, and sprayed onto the garden. Again, this is not the most practical of methods, so it has been further developed and a dried version called Mausdorf Starter is now available from biodynamic suppliers. This can be added to the compost heap, worked into the soil surface, or added to potting media to great beneficial effect. I have used the Mausdorf Starter in my new compost heap at home, and it has really performed well.

∧ Mausdorf Starter can be purchased online from biodynamic suppliers— this cup of the preparation is ready to use.

< Cow manure collected from a local farm is good for adding to a compost heap at an early stage.

Using biodynamic compost

Unlike traditional applications of garden compost, the biodynamic heap produces a potent, lively, and energy-rich soil improver that can be applied in small quantities. As a result of the preparations, it is inoculated with everything that soil, plants, and, in fact, Nature as a whole require. It's not just a once-and-then-forget-about-it addition, however; this is an annual task at least, or every time you harvest a crop. Roughly speaking, one square headed shovel of compost will suffice for about a square meter of garden, but experiment with a little more or less depending on your resources. Once you have applied the compost, scratch it about a bit or run a hoe over the area to work it in a little, and don't forget that there is absolutely no need to dig it in.

∨ My garden early in the season, showing cow manure on the left, and nice fine homemade compost on the right.

Biodynamic Farm

Robert Tilsley is the Head Gardener at Tablehurst Farm, a large biodynamic farm in East Sussex, England. He runs 16 acres (6.5 hectares), which are rotated so that half of the area is always under production, as well as six polytunnels for growing and one for propagation. The soil is a tricky silty loam, with a pH of around 7.0, and has to be worked at just the right time.

On leaving school, Robert trained to be an engineer but, after four years, didn't like the factory environment. He then traveled and spent time volunteering on an organic farm in New Zealand. Once back in England, he decided to train in biodynamic agriculture at Emerson College, where he subsequently worked. He liked the principles of community-based, socially responsible agriculture, and soon realized that this was his path in life.

Robert's foundations and gardening styles are rooted in biodynamic practices. He firmly believes in top-quality husbandry and treating the soil with great respect, using biodynamic preparations and composts to improve it. He does not follow the elemental days because these do not work easily with the commercial side of growing, but believes good husbandry is of the utmost importance. He is aware of, and can observe, the power of the moon's phases and paths in the garden, even if he can't always adhere to these. If he had the luxury of more time, Robert would like to take a more lunar approach, convinced that the moon has a great effect on results.

< Biodynamics on full power; the large garden fields at Tablehurst Farm produce tons of vegetables, and supply the local community.

During his studies, Robert worked for Jane Scotter at Fern Verrow biodynamic farm, in southeast Wales, and regards her as a key influence in his life, along with his work at Tablehurst Farm. He also holds Sarah Raven in high regard, having learned a lot about growing and cooking with unusual vegetable varieties and growing excellent flowers.

Robert gardens for pleasure, thoroughly enjoys the smiles on the faces of customers who buy his produce, and takes great pride in seeing first-class fresh vegetables instantly on the market.

"I garden for pure enjoyment. To work the soil and grow good produce gives me fulfillment."

Garden and farm blend naturally and provide a diverse life for all organisms.

∧ More exotic vegetables are grown in the polytunnels. These allow for growing all year round.

∨ Large wooden barrels are used for mixing the preparations.

CHAPTER 4

Growing for Food

Growing vegetables and fruit for your kitchen is one of the most rewarding tasks for the gardener. There is little to compare with walking into your garden and picking a bowl of fresh salad leaves, a few herbs to flavor it, and a handful of tomatoes, which you are sitting and eating fifteen minutes later. From very small to very large gardens, in cities, villages, and open countryside, there is the potential to grow more produce than you imagined possible. This produce will probably taste better than anything you've ever had before. And, what is more, there is the added bonus that you grew the food yourself.

Deciding What to Grow

A significant range of vegetables can be grown at home, which makes planning your garden a potentially daunting task. If you look through any good seed catalog, you'll notice that there are many types of tomato, lettuce, bean, or pea available, each offering something a little different. Thankfully, the task is not as complicated as it might appear, and here you will find some useful tips for narrowing down the choice.

The first step is quite simple, but the most important. Before making any plans, sit down and make a list of the vegetables and fruit that you like to eat. Next, think about your grocery patterns, what you usually buy, and perhaps even the cost of those items. If you are short of space, or want to make the most of your productive garden, this simple list will help you to grow efficiently and sensibly. I will give you an example from my own garden, which is not very large and needs to be planned well. During the summer we eat a lot of salad, with half of our weekly main meals being leaf-based. Buying good salad in bags is very expensive, and never as satisfying as that which is grown at home, so I concentrate on having plenty of salad on the go (which also includes peas and beans). We also eat a lot of potatoes, but they take up a lot of space and can be tricky to grow in our clay soil. Added to this, potatoes are very reasonable to buy, with some tasty varieties available from local farm shops. With this in mind, I grow a few potatoes for pure satisfaction, but devote far more space to salad crops, which saves me money and cuts down on waste.

Having completed this exercise, it is time to make a plan. Roughly measure your garden and work out the size of the planting beds. What you decide to grow will depend on personal taste, as well as available space, but assume for now that you will grow rows of vegetables spaced at 12in (30cm). This rough guide will help you work out how many different crops you can grow and, therefore, how much seed to buy. In a bed that is 6ft (1.8m) long, you will be able to grow approximately five rows of vegetables, which may all be different or successional sowings of the same crop (see pages 94–5).

What you grow will also depend on your soil type (see page 67). You may be in an area that is perfect for root vegetables or, like me, somewhere in which they struggle a little. If you don't already know your soil type, then ask around, see what local growers say, and read up on the best conditions for your preferred crops (or find out by trial and error). Whatever you decide to grow, be prepared to accept that no two gardens are the same and neither are the seasons. Baffling things will happen each year, causing old reliables to do unusually badly, and supposedly difficult crops to boom.

< Marking out an area for sowing first makes the task much easier.

∧ Runner beans are a good, simple starter crop. They take little space growing up frames and then reward the gardener with lovely flowers followed by bountiful crops.

> Eggplants (aubergines) need a glasshouse or warm climate. They are a very rewarding fruit, however, and worth the extra effort.

> Don't try to do too much too soon. Start simply by growing tomatoes.

Useful tip

A final consideration when deciding what to grow is that, as a beginner, it really does pay to start simply. Growing only salads, or perhaps salads, tomatoes, and a large crop of potatoes, is a great way to start. Always remember: do fewer things well, rather than lots of things badly, and you will be far happier in yourself.

< Lettuce sown direct into warm soil, under a waxing, ascending moon, will respond quickly and soon be ready for harvesting.

Sowing Seed in Beds

Sowing seed directly into prepared soil beds is by far the simplest and least labor-intensive way to raise young plants. As soon as your soil is warm enough after the winter—and this will depend on where you are in the world— you can raise all manner of plants in this way. The best way to tell if the soil is ready is to watch Nature. Weeds will start germinating and the "spring flush" will be apparent in cooler climates.

You'll find that the no-dig gardening approach (see page 64) will provide the perfect conditions for seedlings to thrive. A frequently mulched, fine, and loose soil surface will be light and free draining, and slightly raised after a while, too. By ensuring that any mulch you add to the beds is very well broken down, or sieved, you should need to carry out minimal soil preparation only.

Useful tip

Covering newly sown seed with horticultural fleece or mesh has a number of benefits, including keeping the soil temperature a little higher and protecting against wind and surprise frosts. It also keeps off birds and cats, which, if nothing else, stops them digging about. More specifically, it is good for defending carrots against carrot root fly.

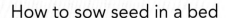

(1) After hoeing off or pulling out any weeds, lightly rake over the soil to ensure the very top surface layer is fine, loose, and free of larger lumps. The sieved lumps can be returned to the compost to further break down.

(5) With the seed in place, mark each row at both ends and use a label noting the seed name and sowing date, ideally labeling at least one row in each group. This will help you to identify seedlings from weeds in the days to come, as well as track the success of your crops.

(2) Lay a bamboo cane, or something similar, where you want to sow the seed. By gently wiggling the cane from side to side you can create a narrow drill in the soft, prepared tilth. Make the drill deep enough to take small seed directly, or use it as a guide for pushing in larger ones like peas further with your finger.

(3) If you are sowing more than one row, then I find it helps to mark out each row in this way first.

(4) *Check your moon calendar for when to sow and remember that the best time for germination is a few days before a full moon.* Tip the seeds into the palm of your hand, take a pinch of seed, and begin to lay them in your drill (following the instructions on the seed packet). Here, I sowed carrot and parsnip, both very different in size. Make sure you sow enough to guarantee good germination, but then thin them out a little later after a few weeks of growing.

(6) Cover the seed lightly by gently dragging over the displaced soil from the drill so that the surface is level again. Water in the seed using either a watering can fitted with a rose attachment or a sprinkler. As an optional final stage, you can cover the seed with some horticultural fleece or mesh. Lay the fleece over the bed and cut it to size, leaving enough spare to allow for later slack for top growth. When the fleece is in place, peg it down and let Nature get to work.

(7) While waiting for the seeds to germinate—and they all vary in the time this takes—water the bed slightly if the soil gets very dry. Peek under the fleece at night to check for slugs and hoe off any weed seedlings between the rows when still small. The fleece can be removed once the second leaves have been produced, but it can also be left on for as long as you wish—just remember to allow some slack for the plants to grow.

Sowing Seed in Containers

While sowing seed directly into beds is the simplest method, sowing in containers for transplanting is often more reliable and certainly more exact. This method allows you to raise individual seedlings quite precisely, in a protected environment, and, if you are lucky enough to own a greenhouse, also with extra warmth. I don't have a greenhouse and use a raised bench made from a stack of transport pallets, which keeps the containers off the ground on a structure that is difficult for marauding molluscs to navigate.

Choosing the best containers

I prefer to use individual cell trays for sowing seed because you can put just one seed in each cell, or two if you have enough, thinning out the weaker specimen on germination. The cells come in various sizes, which means that the larger they are, the longer you can leave the plants in before transplanting. In some cases, you will need to transplant the seedlings when they are still small, so bigger cells are not ideal. However, large seeds like beans require large cells. You may decide to use traditional seed trays with no divisions or to sow into pots. This is fine, but you'll have to go through the process of "pricking out" the young seedlings, which will add yet another stage and more stress, so I advise against it.

Preparing potting media

There are lots of different potting media to choose from. Specific seed sowing mixes are available, but are not necessary. A good organic potting compost will do well, but be aware that loam-based potting composts may sit a little wet if over watered. I prefer to make my own potting media by sieving very well-rotted garden compost. I first screen it by laying a 1-in (2.5-cm) mesh over a wheelbarrow and loading it in. I then push the compost through a soil sieve as and when I need it. As this is the same surface that I would sow directly into on the beds, this seems sensible and works well.

< Seeds sown in pots of any size will benefit from a horticultural fleece cover to protect them and also provide a warm microclimate.

∧ Individual cell trays are perfect for sowing seed and accurately raising individual plants for planting out directly.

How to sow seed in cell trays

(1) Working on a table or workbench, make a pile of sieved garden compost or potting media.

(2) Keeping the cell tray flat, sprinkle compost over the tray until all of the cells are filled, with a little extra proud of the surface.

(3) Gently tamp down the surface of the compost with the palm of your hand, before brushing away the excess material.

(4) Use a special dibble (dibber) or pencil to make shallow holes suitable for the size of your seeds in the center of each cell.

(5) *Remember to check your moon calendar for when to sow and bear in mind that the best time for germination is a few days before a full moon.* Tip the seeds into your hand—in this case, beets (beetroot)—and start putting a seed into each hole. Here, I put three seeds in each cell so that the beets would form a nice clump when maturing.

(6) When all of the cells have been sown, gently fill each hole using the sharp end of the dibble or pencil.

(7) Remember to add a label stating the plant's name and the sowing date.

(8) Finally, water the seeds using a watering can with a rose attachment and put the cell tray in a safe place for the seeds to get working.

> If you use a lunar calendar to choose the optimum time for transplanting young plants, you should find that they establish quickly.

After germination

This is the exciting stage: waiting for the seeds to germinate. I cover my trays with horticultural fleece, in the same way as I cover the soil when sowing seed directly, because this creates a little microclimate and also protects the seedlings a little from the elements. If you have space, place the seeds in a warmer spot to speed things up—a window sill is good, as is a greenhouse. If possible, supplying bottom heat is best. You can buy heated blankets for this purpose, but the best method I have seen is a large box filled with 35 cubic feet (1 cubic meter) of fresh manure, with a board over the top, and the seed tray placed on that. The heat generated by the manure as it breaks down is startlingly good.

Potting on and transplanting

When the seedlings have been growing for a while, you will notice roots poking out of the bottom of the cells. This means that the seedlings are nearly ready for potting on or transplanting into the open garden. The optimum time is when you can hold the base of the seedling and gently remove the whole plant without the compost breaking up. Don't leave the seedlings too long, however, as the stress caused by low nutrients, the potting compost drying out, and insufficient space can make them bolt and spoil. When it is time to transplant the young plants, remember to check your moon calendar—you are aiming to plant under a descending moon and on the correct elemental day.

< Planting cell-raised young plants in a loose, no-dig bed, which has been mulched with garden compost, is simple, fast, and effective.

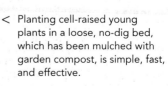

< Healthy young plants ready for planting. Remember to check for good rooting first.

∧ In a sunny glasshouse, seedlings will germinate quickly and thrive due to the added protection.

Useful tip

Seed raised in containers still responds well to the influences of the moon, so do pay attention to this when sowing. If your compost heap is not biodynamic, then you can add Mausdorf Starter (see page 78) to your sieved compost before potting. This will greatly benefit your seedlings and their future life as plants.

Successful Planting Groups

It is quite acceptable only to sow or plant rows of vegetables at their correct spacing and at the optimum time. This is a nice simple approach, and perhaps best for the beginner, but it is also possible to plant in clever combinations and to plant crops in different places every year or so. These methods have the benefit of making the most of available space, acting as a pest deterrent, and avoiding disease build-up in the soil. It can also give you an opportunity to have unconventional planting fun.

Some vegetables mature very quickly, while some like to take their time, so it seems sensible to consider this when sowing for two reasons. Firstly, early sown lettuce that is harvested by mid-summer can be followed in the same spot by a winter-maturing crop, thus giving two crops per year from the same area. Secondly, some vegetables like parsnips take all season to mature, so it is possible to raise a fast crop of radishes between the rows. This technique is known as intercropping and is a very efficient way to make the most of your garden (see the *Crops and their companion plants* table below for some successful combinations).

Companion planting

The practice of companion planting has been in existence for years, but I have to admit that it's not something I have taken much notice of. I also note that a legendary organic grower with decades of experience, Charles Dowding, only really recommends using a few combinations in his book *Vegetable Course*, having found after years of trials

∧ Marigolds planted with lettuce not only look complementary, but help to deter aphids too.

Crops and their companion plants

Main Plant	Companion Plant	Results
Carrot, parsnip	Radish, onion, leek, mint	Sow radish between the rows as a fast intercrop. Scallions (spring onions) or leeks can deter carrot root fly. Mint has a similar deterrent effect.
Tomato	French marigold (*Tagetes patula*), basil, chives	Planting basil at the base of tomatoes improves their flavor, deters aphids, and is the source of a great Caprese salad. Marigolds and chives also deter aphids.
Cabbage, kale, cauliflower	Nasturtium, mint, lettuce	Nasturtium is loved by the Cabbage White Butterfly caterpillar, so can be planted in sacrifice. Mint deters flea beetles. Plant early lettuce between them as a fast intercrop.
Climbing beans	Sweet pea (*Lathyrus odoratus*)	Highly scented sweet peas will attract pollinators to the beans, as well as provide lovely flowers.
Fava (broad) beans	Summer savory (*Satureja hortensis*)	Summer savory helps deter blackfly, which love fava beans about as much as I do.
Garlic	Carrot, beet (beetroot)	Either can be sown between the rows of maturing garlic in mid-summer as an intercrop.

that many do not work. The theory is that certain plants deter certain pests, perhaps because they are very pungent. One combination that Charles Dowding does use is to plant French marigolds (*Tagetes patula*) alongside indoor tomatoes. The marigolds deter aphids due to the fragrance of their foliage, while looking rather nice, too. For me, though, successful pest control comes back to the root of biodynamics, and that is diversity through good husbandry.

Apart from these observations, why separate vegetable plants from ornamental ones? I think much enjoyment is to be had from raising a few potatoes at the back of a border, covering a gazebo with climbing beans, or harvesting rhubarb from a decorative corner. So, don't be afraid to mix things up, experiment, and have fun, because each garden is very different—and so are its gardeners!

Rotating crops

Crop rotation is a very traditional agricultural practice that dates back hundreds of years. Farmers first adopted a three-year cycle, with the third year being fallow, until new innovations led to a four-year cycle with no fallow year. This approach made its way into horticulture and involves dividing the garden into four sections, growing set family groups in each quarter, and moving them around each season so that the soil sees the same crop every fourth year.

Rotating crops can be quite complicated and needs a lot of planning on your part to get it right. It also means you have to grow and eat everything needed for rotation and assumes you have the space and, what's more, the inclination to do so. I have tried it in the past, both in my workplace and at home, and have found it to be deeply stressful and often confusing.

For me there is only one strong reason for rotating crops, and that is to avoid a build-up of disease. I don't think it's necessary to rotate crops in order to provide for them if the soil is well fed. I have also known gardeners who grow the same thing in the same spot for years without a problem. The sensible approach is to move things about and to try and avoid growing the same crop in the same spot the following season. This is something I have always done when growing vegetables, but only out of a vague notion that crop rotation seemed "fussy." So, I was pleased to learn that Charles Dowding feels the same and also gardens in this way. Dowding advises that you try to leave a two-year gap between growing plants of the same family in the same spot, and that a four-year rotation is very hard to achieve in a small garden.

The answer comes down, as always, to good husbandry. Variety will keep the ecology of your garden broad, which in turn will lead to healthy growth and lots of beneficial insects and animals. Be organic, observe and follow the moon, feed the soil well, and improve it biodynamically. The result will be strong plants that produce extremely well and, what's more, taste fantastic. You will also be less stressed—and the importance of this cannot be underestimated when tending a garden.

Tips to avoid disease build-up

* Feed your soil well, either with organic garden compost, well-rotted manure, biodynamic compost, or all three.
* Apply the BD 500 preparation to your soil twice a year.
* Apply a different organic matter after each harvest, and try to vary the type you use a little.
* Move your crops about each time, without too much of a plan, avoiding the same spot for two years if you can.
* Encourage as much wildlife into your garden as possible, especially birds and hedgehogs.
* Keep weeds under control, as they can harbor all sorts of nasties.

Keeping Your Salad Bowl Full All Year

Whether you're a novice or a professional there is one crop that we can all grow reliably, easily, and quickly—salad. Not only are salad leaves expensive to buy—the cost of one small bag buys enough seed for a season—but often when you open the bag, a strange, unnatural smell is given off. This smell is created by nothing that grows and leaves me deeply suspicious—and less keen to eat it. In contrast, salad picked from the garden, minutes before it is served, is so different, so rich in taste and vibrancy that I can't get enough and long for it when I don't have it. So, how do you keep it going all year round?

Successional sowing

The most common mistake in vegetable growing is sowing seed all at once, resulting in a single batch of produce. This can be overcome by a technique called successional sowing, which can be applied to both open beds and containers, and makes total sense. This method involves sowing small batches of seed at intervals, depending on speed of growth and use, from as much as weekly to perhaps monthly. For example, two small rows of sugar peas (mangetout) followed by two more a month later will spread out the harvest time and reduce waste. A single, full lettuce plant will provide enough leaves to equal a purchased bag. If the leaves are picked while it grows, then this quantity can be increased still further. It is easy to work out, therefore, that seven lettuce plants will provide a bag a day, which is a lot. I like variety, and so choose several favorites to grow all summer.

When sown directly into beds that are 3ft (1m) wide, just before each full moon, I find that one row of each variety, spaced correctly, is more than enough for a couple of people for several weeks if picked correctly. You can, of course, raise the seedlings in cells, which is more precise and wastes little seed. A tray of 24 cells

< Traditional "hearting" lettuce plants can be harvested by removing leaves from the base as they grow. In this way, they produce leaves for several months, which helps avoid a glut of salad and gives a daily supply from a small area. Remove the leaves by breaking them downward close to the stem.

∧ Growing a variety of salad leaves allows for a lovely, mixed bowl of salad that can be different every day.

> Allowing leaves to "heart up" results in bumper harvests, but potential wastage.

each month will again produce quite a lot of leaf once planted out, but in both cases be sure that the seed choice is correct.

The choice of seed will be greatly influenced by the type of salad you enjoy, but that in turn will have an impact on the harvesting techniques used. Many types of lettuce that "heart" up can be grown and the lower leaves harvested over a long spell. As the leaves are removed, a stalk develops, resulting in little salad trees, but they will produce for weeks. Alternatively, you can scissor off the leaves of some seed mixes (known as cut-and-come-again salads) when they are young. This type of salad requires weekly sowings. If you take a little care in the selection of your salad varieties, then you'll soon discover what you prefer and how you need to manage the sowing.

Growing winter salad

Winter salad takes a little more thought, unless you are lucky enough to live in a Mediterranean or tropical climate. Oriental salads and arugula (rocket) can survive rather cold conditions, with regular frosting and outside temperatures of 14°F (-10°C) if protected. An unheated glasshouse or polytunnel provides good protection, but at the very least I suggest you use a hooped cloche with nursery-grade polythene or professional horticultural fleece. Protection such as this keeps the worst of the elements from battering the leaves, raises the temperature just a degree or so more, and on mild days provides a nice growing environment. You can't expect such rapid growth in winter, however, so simply plant a little more, or eat and savor a little less, but do enjoy year-round salads.

Care and Maintenence

So far, your time and attention have been focused on preparing the garden for vegetables, raising seed, and planting out your precious young plants. Now you have to concentrate on looking after them, which can make or break the will of even the hardiest of individuals. I find it is all down to timeliness and good planning. There is nothing worse than raising seeds to a final crop only to find the produce is of poor quality, woody and tasteless, or has been eaten by bugs—I find both so frustrating because I know they are the result of bad husbandry.

So how do you overcome these situations and have a pleasurable experience when growing? Once again, I think the key is to start simply, with a limited range of vegetable types, so that you can concentrate on growing them well. It's a bit like playing an old space invaders game, in that the game begins slowly and with only a few UFOs to blast, but, as it goes on, everything speeds up and there are targets everywhere. Experience improves your skill at the game and it's the same with growing vegetables, which is much harder than ornamental gardening. With good, well-prepared soil, young plants in the ground, and a few seedlings germinating there are several things to bear in mind for their future care.

Thinning

Thinning is a crucial operation when you are sowing seeds directly into open beds. This is because it is always wise to sow seed more densely than the eventual crop should be, as you will have some insurance against germination problems, the odd pest nibble, and accidental weeding out. The eventual size of the plants will probably be bigger than the spacing of the seedlings, so you have to thin out the seedlings to provide enough room for growth and to cut down on potential disease through lack of air movement.

Thinning out seedlings

① After strong germination these young spinach plants are too close together. Indentify the stronger specimens in a row and remove the weaker or unnecessary ones. Always check recommended spacings when thinning.

② Remove the thinned plants, root and all, while using your fingers to "protect" the roots of remaining plants when pulling. If carefully removed, they can sometimes be transplanted for filling gaps.

At that exciting moment when your seedlings first show their heads you will be able to get an idea of their success rate—and, hopefully, it is very good. All good seed packets advise on the eventual density of the plants, so check the packet for recommendations, and, as soon as several sets of leaves have developed, you can get to work. It may be very clear that the spacing between each juvenile plant needs to be 6in (15cm), but, in the case of clump-forming plants such as carrot and beets (beetroot), the spacing is more down to judgment. As root vegetables can do well growing close together, I find it helps to have in mind the eventual size of the root. If a small carrot needs ¾in (20mm) of space, then I go through the seedlings, ensuring they all have that much space and pulling out the weaker looking ones.

Thinning out also improves the eventual harvest. It will be stronger and more vibrant, and less likely to have been nibbled by pests hiding within. It is also a good way for you to get up close to, and have an idea of, the success and health of your plants.

Watering

Water is, of course, key to the survival of all life forms. It is also through this element that the moon imparts it's great power and influence. Vegetables need good supplies of water to do well. Indeed, many things can go wrong in a dry spell, but above all your vegetables simply will not grow much. How much you need to water will depend on the climate in which you garden, but this in turn will influence what you grow.

Water is precious, and should not be squandered, so we should try to garden with this in mind. In the United Kingdom it is very common to have an entire season of growing with only one or two weeks that really need total irrigation. Spending time developing a good, un-dug soil structure will reduce the need to water, while a good layer of organic matter at the top will further aid this. The trick is to grow to suit your climate, whether blisteringly hot, or mild and damp, because it is a fool's errand trying to "fight the site," as I myself have learned.

In the afternoon and evening, water is drawn down to Earth, and taken into the

∨ Water only when necessary, but always ensure that vegetables have a good supply. Soil absorbs water fully in the late afternoon, under a waning moon, but don't let plants suffer if there is a hot spell in a waxing moon.

Having a good selection of tools is important, but there needn't be too many. Of this collection, I only really use the hoe, soil rake, and trowel regularly.

soil more effectively. If you have to water, aim for this time, but don't let plants suffer to achieve this. In his book *Garden Myths and Misconceptions*, Charles Dowding points out that science has proven that there is no risk to plants if you water them in direct sun. The old tale that it scorches the leaves is not true, so if you see a need to water, then do it right away.

The main aim is to keep moisture levels available to the plant at a steady and reliable level. Soaking and drying out is a stress, and asking for trouble, so try and be consistent. It is as easy to over water as it is to let things dry out, so, if you are not sure, just part the soil for a few inches and see what is going on below. Often there is enough held under a dry cap and you won't need to water as often as you think.

Controlling weeds

Weeding is the bane of every gardener's life, taking many hours of our time in a thankless routine of clearing, growing, clearing, growing. As native or naturalized plants, weeds are strong, fast, and often the cause of vegetable failure through competition, pests, disease, or a combination of all three. While I enjoy weeding, find it therapeutic thinking time, and am always pleased with the results, I never have enough time to be that luxurious and would rather spend it growing more of a range of crops.

For this reason weeding is the first task that you must learn to keep on top of, and there is actually a very easy way to do this—use a garden hoe. The hoe has existed for hundreds of years in a number of different forms, and is a way of lightly cultivating the surface of the soil. The aim with this tool is to cut through the roots of weeds (which are by definition only unwanted plants) just below the surface of the soil, causing them to die quickly. Hoeing is a very effective way to control the weed problem. Timing, however, is critical for this operation, but well worth getting right, as I have found that you can hoe off emergent seedlings throughout a large vegetable garden in 30 minutes. If you leave the weeds for another week, then the task is doubled; leave them for a month and it becomes a whole day's work, which is very daunting. Month-old weeds will also have set seed, only creating future problems, whereas a weekly hoe means that they will die before seeding, resulting in a widespread reduction in weeds over time.

Hoeing

To make the most of a hoe, it is worth planning the garden accordingly. Make sure that directly sown rows of seed are far enough apart for you to run a hoe between them, and that the same is considered when planting. Narrow beds will also make hoeing easier, allowing you to reach everything from the path without standing on your precious soil. In doing this you will easily be able to run the hoe around, which is best done when the sun is hot and the ground dry. A

seedling that is one week old will not last 15 minutes when cut off on a hot, dry day.

Choose your hoe carefully and, if you can, try it out before buying. Like everything, the better ones are more expensive, but this is the tool to stretch your budget on. You will also need to sharpen the hoe regularly because, like anything that cuts, it is significantly more efficient when sharp. There are many types available, but the best is the oscillating or stirrup hoe, which actually makes the job easy.

You must also be sure to keep the soil weed-free when not in use, which means running the hoe over vacant beds as well, or perhaps covering them with black plastic when they are empty for longer periods. Plastic is a great way to control weeds, but, if you are gardening biodynamically, it does rather shut off the surface from those penetrating solar and lunar rays.

It is also important to look outside the boundaries of your garden, and be sure that there isn't a crop of weeds going to seed just next door. If this is the case, then you might be able to arrange to control them before this happens.

Routine hoeing when weeds are still small helps you keep on top of them and has allowed these young parsnips to establish without competition.

Pests, Diseases, and Disorders

I have not always been an organic grower, mostly because I knew no better, but also out of laziness. However, I have grown organically for a while now and found that simply striving to grow healthy plants is more than enough to cope with most problems. More and more it is being proven that a diverse habitat is the key to pest and disease control, not the use of chemicals, which only creates false conditions.

∧ Physical barriers are the best start when tackling pests. On the left, a fine horticultural mesh stops very small insects, while on the right, netting protects against larger animals.

Bugs and beasties

Also known as pests, this wide cohort of marauding creatures can ruin your efforts overnight, and be hard to control, which is why it is so tempting to reach for the massive arsenal of chemicals that are available. But be strong, resist, and do it organically, because you really don't want to be consuming such toxins. These will also have major ramifications on all the life in your garden.

I recently heard biodynamic growing described as "the most advanced form of organic growing, using animal systems to create the perfect environment." This phrase refers to biodiversity, and the creation of ecosystems and living communities that self-manage, and we are part of that system. So how does this work in practice? Here are some simple guidelines to start you off:

Molluscs: Slugs and snails are a major pest and can take out a row of seedlings overnight. The best method of control is to go out after dark and find them, especially when it's damp. You can squash them but, if you don't want to do that, just put them in a bucket and deposit them in a hedge over 300ft (100m) away. Slugs and snails will also be controlled by a range of birds, as well as hedgehogs and frogs, so be sure to encourage these wild creatures into your garden.

Aphids: These can be black, green, or anything else between. Most plants that are growing healthily will outgrow an aphid problem, but not always. I usually blast them off with a jet of water, delivered through a trigger attachment on the end of a garden hose. I find that this is very effective and generally solves the problem if it is caught early enough. It is also worth knowing that wasps are really useful in our battle against aphids. They harvest aphids and take them back to their nest to feed to the young larvae, so are not such a nuisance after all.

Light netting stops birds destroying these brassicas, and is easily laid over the crop when working narrow vegetable beds.

∧ Caterpillars can cause a lot of damage very quickly. Keep a close eye out for them, and remove them immediately—in this case by removing the leaves with the little nasties attached.

Beneficial wildlife

Never forget that in the natural balance you are striving to achieve as an organic or biodynamic gardener, there will always be wildlife around. Any action you take might discourage them, and they are your best friends, so leave them somewhere to hide, feed, and feel safe. Try to leave some patches of weed, which will also give ingredients for organic teas. Don't tidy up too much, but leave discreet piles of woody prunings, logs, and dead growth through summer and winter, which are all places loved by visiting wildlife.

Caterpillars: These naughty chaps can be very voracious feeders and, again, can ruin a crop in no time. If you see foliage being eaten, and there is no sign of slug or snail slime, then it is likely to be the work of caterpillars. Again, remove and squish them, or throw them to the birds. Plants that are prone to this problem, chiefly the Brassica family, should be netted throughout their growing life to keep the adult butterflies away. A fine horticultural mesh such as Enviromesh® is required for this.

Birds: Some crops are very prone to bird damage, particularly brassicas and peas. Netting against the Cabbage White Butterfly will keep birds off, but young pea shoots should be protected while getting under way.

Rabbits: There is little point trying to garden if you have a rabbit problem. They are persistent and have expensive tastes, so will quickly eat your favorite crops. Rabbits need to be kept out of the garden using a fence of small-gauge wire that is at least 3ft (1m) high and buried 10in (25cm) deep. Otherwise, they will certainly jump over or burrow under it, and your efforts will be wasted. Also be careful not to fence rabbits into your garden, as this will focus their efforts in just one direction.

Diseases

Diseases and fungal problems are almost always caused by the wrong growing conditions. A healthy plant does not tend to be susceptible and, even if it does pick something up, is usually able to grow through the issue.

Diseases show up in many forms, but are usually easy to spot because the plants do not look as you would expect. Leaves may wilt quickly, blotches may crop up, a gray-white covering might develop, or you may find fruit developing similar issues and even falling off.

On discovering a disease problem you must first ask what conditions have caused it. If you were constantly ill yourself, then a doctor would want to know about your diet, lifestyle, and general well-being before making an assessment—and it is the same for plants. In most cases you will find that the optimum growing conditions have somehow been compromised, and that the weakened or stressed plant is not fit to defend itself.

Most diseases and molds occur in damp conditions, where the airflow is poor and the spores can travel or "germinate" easily in water droplets. Even in the height of summer a glasshouse can get too damp and must always have ventilation. Leaves that dry out for a spell once a day are far less likely to develop damp-loving problems, but at the same time don't let your plants wilt, as this is also a stressful time when their defences are weak.

Both inside and outside, too much foliage can also be a problem, as this inhibits airflow during wet spells. Growth can be abundant due to the moist conditions, but this in turn can lead to related problems. Growing plants at their suggested spacing will help with this, and is another good reason for keeping weeds at bay, as they can become very competitive and harbor all sorts of nasties. At the first sign of damp-related problems it is a good idea to thin any foliage where possible, having removed weeds first. This technique involves cutting off leaves with a sharp knife or hand pruners (secateurs) to allow more airflow and is especially good for tomatoes, for example. In the glasshouse, it is best to do this after a period of ventilation, as open wounds may be infected with spores, which can travel far more easily when wet.

As you tend your garden, always be watchful and keep an eye out for irregularities, especially during wet spells. On spotting what looks like a disease, don't panic; simply remove the leaves in question, or the whole plant, and take it away for identification. Once you have found out what the problem is, you can try to understand the cultural issues that caused it and then rectify them quickly. In most cases, if you spot diseases early and remove the material, the conditions can be altered quickly and the problem kept at bay.

Many growers have found that homemade comfrey tea (see page 53) is wonderful for controlling diseases, and there is research showing it to be beneficial. By using this organic tea as a routine part of your maintenance program, you will not only feed the plants, but provide disease protection too.

Disorders

In a healthy, well-fed garden you shouldn't experience any disorders, which are usually caused by nutrient deficiencies. These are more common in container-grown plants if the potting media is lacking in nutrients or these have run low. The most obvious symptoms are a general

∧   While growth is strong and healthy, there is plenty of space for air to circulate in this glasshouse, keeping the chance of damp-loving diseases to a minimum.

yellowing of the foliage; slow, weak growth; leaves with green veins and yellow areas in between; or green young leaves and yellow older ones. Nutrient deficiencies tend to be slow to develop, and take a little longer to fix, but this can be achieved using several applications of one of the natural feeds detailed on pages 52–5. However, it is better to try to avoid this problem in the first place by continually feeding your soil with good garden compost and by using the range of biodynamic preparations available.

Harvesting

Harvesting your vegetables is a time of great joy and excitement. That pleasure does not diminish with the years, and there is always a new variety to try out or an experimental method to test. It may just be three precious apples, a small pot of carrots, or an entire orchard and allotment, but in all cases these have been the focus of love and devotion. To get a plant to harvesting stage has taken effort, skill, perhaps some luck, and most certainly time, so we should make the best effort to harvest it correctly too.

∧ Carrots picked in the afternoon, when the Earth is inhaling, ideally on a root day, will contain more moisture and taste better.

< Drying in the sun, these onions are harvested on a descending root day for the best possible storage and taste.

Work always with good husbandry in mind, and a thought to the health of the plants. Make clean cuts using sharp hygienic tools when snipping, and pick fruit when the plant gives it freely. Tomatoes and apples don't need a hefty tug when they are ready, while cutting beans on a small scale means you are less likely to damage the plant.

If you are gardening by the moon, then remember it will have a strong influence on the volume of water in a plant (including the fruit). The few days prior to a full moon will see a powerful lift in moisture levels, so resulting in plumper, juicier fruit (in contrast with a new moon, which has a much less powerful pull). Plants that produce their crop above the ground will be full of sap—for example, tomatoes and apples will be at their fullest near a full moon and with all Nature's forces on their side. When the moon has less power, then root vegetables will be giving less to top growth and thus in a position to fill out more.

To focus in even further is to consider the elemental days, which are an important part of biodynamic gardening. Maria Thun's work highlighted that the good cultivation of plants right through to harvesting has an impact on both taste and storage success. For example, she found that a root vegetable harvested on a root day could be stored in a healthy condition for a long period, whereas it would develop fungal issues and have a poor taste if brought in on the wrong day.

Bear in mind, though, that there also have to be practical considerations when harvesting, in that some produce is ready when it's ready. It is always worth taking on any task knowing the optimum time in which to do it, while at the same time being aware that you can do anything at any time, although this may well have an influence on the results. It would be silly to leave fruit to rot on the plant because the next fruit day is in seven days, yet it is entirely possible to look at a moon calendar and lift your potato crop on a root day. Remember, too, that the weather may also have an impact on harvesting times, or simply life, so the important thing is to aim for the best

moment, but not to be ruled by it. You will not be effective if you work in the garden in a state of stress, and the power of gardening with conscious intent will be eroded.

At home I harvest salad on an almost daily basis due to the level of consumption and a desire for it to be fresh from the plant. I aim to pick at some stage in the morning when the Earth's exhalation allows the leaves to fill with moisture, but I don't always achieve this. I do, however, maintain a very strong sense of happiness and satisfaction from eating completely chemical-free leaves that have a wonderful flavor and which I have grown from seed in rich, healthy soil and picked fresh that day.

∨ Apples will not only taste nicer, but also store better if they are consistently tended and harvested on fruit days.

Growing Herbs

Rather like salads, herbs are one of those items that are very expensive to buy and yet quite simple to grow. In fact, some herbs like fennel and thyme are so prolific that they'll always be with you once you've started growing them. Many of us use herbs for cooking or making fragrances, and are prepared to buy jars of dried leaves that then sit around for months or years, retaining only a distant hint of their former pungency. However, it is easy to grow some fresh herbs to use in the kitchen. I have found that the small range of herbs I use regularly can be grown in a few pots outside the kitchen door or in a small bed somewhere in the garden.

When herbs are picked as needed they are not only fresher, but have another layer of fragrance that makes for a richer flavor in food. They also make nice ornamental plants, adding flowers and fragrance to the garden. It is delightful to brush past some rosemary growing alongside paths or steps, and personally I can't help but pick the odd leaf to sniff when passing sage.

There is a common misconception that herbs need poor, dry, or sandy soil to grow well and that they are difficult in damp conditions. At Sissinghurst Castle, in England, where I once worked, the soil is heavy clay and very wet in the winter. At the bottom of the garden, where the soil laid heaviest and wettest, was the herb garden, which contained a vast range of culinary and medicinal plants. I have discovered that while herbs often come from hot, dry countries, they grow very well in more temperate conditions. I have also found that if they are regularly clipped for foliage, then they need a moist, nutrient-rich soil to produce plenty of vigorous leaves. For this reason, I believe that they can be grown in a wide range of situations, but, as for many plants, it is best to avoid an area that lays wet for long periods and is exposed to very cold conditions. Herbs also grow very well in containers, a subject that is covered in detail on pages 148–9.

The selection given in the table opposite is just the tip of the iceberg, as there are many herbs that can be grown at home and in a relatively small area. This year I have limited most of my herbs to containers, but next year I am planning to plant up a small, south-facing bank with a variety of favorites. In my chosen spot, they will have optimum conditions: nice, nutritious clay, improved with organic garden compost, and a free-draining, south-facing site. An added bonus is that the herbs will be next to a flight of steps, making them easy to harvest and fragrant with every passing.

< Fennel is not only useful, providing seeds and fragrant tips for culinary use, but it is also an attractive ornamental garden plant, which is enjoyed by insects as much as humans.

Basil (*Ocimum basilicum*)

Basil is native to the dry tropical regions of Asia and Africa. As an annual or short-lived perennial it is quite tender and needs a little more care when growing. The leaves can be green or purple, and intensely fragrant, which I love in salads. Outside it needs a sunny, sheltered spot that is not too wet; otherwise, it does very well in pots. Basil will thrive inside when given good, loamy soil and plenty of heat. The strong scent also makes it a good companion plant for warding off pests.

Fennel (*Foeniculum vulgare*)

Native to stony wastes, often coastal in Asia and Southern Europe, fennel is a stately herb with aromatic, feathery foliage and soft, but striking, yellow flower heads. A good addition to borders, as well as herb gardens, it will seed freely and never leave home. The leaves are good chopped in salads and the seeds added to breads.

Rosemary (*Rosmarinus officinalis*)

Native to dry, rocky, Mediterranean areas, rosemary is now available in many cultivated varieties. It is a medium-sized shrub, with very fragrant leaves. A range of different flower colors make it an attractive garden plant, and it can be grown in many soil conditions, as well as in containers.

Sage (*Salvia officinalis*)

Sage is another native of dry areas, with evergreen leaves that range in color from golden through green to purple, depending on the variety. Like rosemary, it has very fragrant leaves, makes a good ornamental specimen, and is happy in open ground or pots.

Italian parsley (*Petroselinum crispum var. neapolitanum*)

Flat-leaved or Italian parsley is a strongly aromatic herbaceous biennial that is great in salads and fragrant cooking. One plant provides a lot of foliage, but it's worth having a few on the go. Native to Southern European grasslands, it does well in open ground, but also in containers. It's a favorite of mine and I always have it.

Useful tip

For the best-tasting herbs, remember to harvest on the correct elemental day. For example, harvest leafy herbs such as sage and basil on a leaf day; fennel seed on a fruit/seed day; and edible flowers, such as lavender, nasturtiums, and borage, on a flower day.

Growing Fruit

Many people overlook growing fruit, perhaps because this is regarded as the domain of large walled gardens or orchards. However, there are fruit-growing options to suit almost every location, which will add a further layer of interest and productivity to your garden. Fruit is often mistaken for being a specialist crop, and therefore complicated, but it really isn't. You only have to taste apples from a long-abandoned tree in an old orchard to realize that they can be wonderful even when the tree is left alone. To cover fruit well would require chapters, so I aim here to raise awareness and hopefully kindle interest.

< Growing fruit is an option for all gardeners, and is wonderfully rewarding.

Tree fruit

Fruiting trees allow you to grow a variety of delicious produce, from apples and pears to cherries, figs, quinces, medlars, mulberries, and plums, to name but a small selection. However, what many people forget is that fruit trees are also attractive. Many have given rise to ornamental favorites, while the fruiting varieties have stunning spring flower displays, good structural habits, and, of course, finish with fruits.

Small trees can bring height and additional interest to a vegetable garden, without casting competing shade, while large trees can be used to provide boundary screening and wind protection. With a little instruction, and some good reference books, it is within everyone's ability to prune and train fruit trees for improved production, but also as structural features against walls, sheds, and fences. Even if you are limited to a balcony or terrace, there is a fruit tree that will grow in a container against a wall, take up little space, and produce a handful of the most precious, mouth-watering apples. Fortunately, too, there are varieties of every type of fruit that can be grown biodynamically—in fact, they prefer to be grown in this way.

Selecting which fruit to grow is the most important decision, and will determine your levels of success. Most fruit has been subjected to widespread breeding and development so that some is suited to intensive chemical farming only, while other fruit is suited to the organic way. The tree that produces the fruit will have been grafted onto a rootstock, with the combinations used giving different results. The same apple, for example, can be grafted onto a vigorous rootstock, which allows it to become a full-sized "standard" tree, or on to a dwarfing rootstock that allows it to reach just 6ft (1.8m). Another consideration is disease resistance, at which some varieties do much better. Time has proven which varieties stand up well to diseases, such as apple scab, and these are the ones that are most suited to a natural way of growing. In any case, it is best to seek the advice of a very good specialist nursery. I have found that if the nursery also supplies commercial growers, the staff often have detailed knowledge.

Where to situate your fruit tree will need some careful thought and is best decided prior to buying the trees. Small trees will have little impact upon your vegetable garden if planted

There are fruit trees for the smallest of corners. They can be easily grown against a shed, trellis, or wall.

within it, but a large one will root through and create dry shade. Try and place large trees where they will not cast heavy shade on your garden or require lots of moisture. Ideally, next to your compost heap is a good location because the tree will keep the heap shaded, while enjoying the nutrients that leach down.

Your fruit tree will thrive in a nice, no-dig, biodynamic soil. It can grow freely into the natural soil, without getting its roots chopped routinely by cultivation, and will benefit from the diverse nutrients. For many years, I have dug a hole just big enough for the root-ball, and don't agree that a large hole needs preparing, because the sooner the tree gets going in the conditions it has to live in, so much the better. Adding a stake is important for the first year or two, but this need protrude no more than 20in (50cm) from the ground for a tree of up to 6ft (1.8m). The

aim is to give it basal support while it roots, allowing the stem to flex and thicken—long stakes just delay this process.

Water the new tree according to the weather, once a day for two weeks in dry spells, and once a week after that. Trees that are planted in the winter rarely need watering unless the spring is unusually dry.

Post-planting care consists of pruning, training, and feeding. Pruning will depend on whether the specimen is free standing or being trained to a structure, so it is best to seek out some tuition or a good book for this. Routine mulching and the application of preparation BD 500 will supply enough feed, but a foliar spray of organic tea and BD 501 will greatly benefit the tree as the fruits develop. Container-grown fruit will do better if given liquid tea feeds once a month, in addition to foliar sprays.

Grapes are well suited to biodynamic cultivation, and this sweet dessert variety is a delight to taste.

Soft fruit

Soft fruit usually encompasses all fruit not grown on trees, such as strawberries that are herbaceous, raspberries that are borne on canes, and currants that grow in the form of a shrub. The range is quite large, including all manner of fruits, and it provides options for large, small, and tiny gardens.

The selection and cultivation requirements of soft fruit are much the same as for tree fruit. You are aiming to select disease-resistant varieties where possible and to maintain the nutritious content of the soil by continuing to care for it well. Soft fruit particularly enjoys an application of comfrey tea (see page 53), which is high in the potassium needed for flower and fruit production. A similar effect can be achieved by lightly dressing the soil surface with clean wood ash from house fires or bonfires.

Birds can be a problem when growing soft fruit and many gardeners obsess about netting the fruit. However, loose netting can trap birds, quickly killing them, whereas well-made fruit cages don't have that effect and so can be better. Remember, too, that birds are a natural predator of pests, a significant part of the ecosystem, and also need feeding, so consider sharing your harvest with them. If you need to reduce their activity, you could try hanging out old compact disks, noisy wind chimes, strips of foil, or anything else that might unsettle them. You should then find that you don't lose your entire fruit crop to hungry birds and there is enough for everyone.

Soft fruits for your garden

Strawberries
(*Fragaria x ananassa*)

These little fruits are possibly the most delightful, rewarding, and happy plants you can grow, being full of summer and sweetness. Grown well in open beds, they can be produced in large numbers with relatively little space. As the name suggests, they do best sitting on a layer of straw as they develop, which stops the fruits rotting on the ground and being eaten by bugs.

They are a very good fruit to grow in containers and hanging baskets, because these allow the plants to trail and spill down the container's sides. Special strawberry planters provide many slots for maximum productivity, and these can be replicated at home in a number of ingenious ways. Consider growing both early and late varieties in order to prolong the fruiting season.

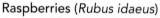

Raspberries (*Rubus idaeus*)

A special favorite of mine, raspberries are grown on canes that are two years old or more. They can be grown in small clumps, but are best cultivated in rows where they can be supported by wires or tied in to a framework. For best results, they need to be kept young, which you can do by cutting back the old stems right to the ground. Raspberries like a good, fertile soil.

Currants (*Ribes species*)
and gooseberries (*Ribes uva-crispum*)

These are produced on low, tight shrubs that can be grown as individual specimens without the need for support, but can also be trained to walls or wire frames for control. They are quite well suited to small gardens, or the corner of a raised bed, and will grow very well in large pots if well fed.

Rambling and climbing berries
(*Rubus species*)

This group of fruit consists of the wide range of blackberries, mixed hybrid berries, loganberries, wineberries, and tayberries. They bear their fruit on arching stems and require support to keep them under control. Some of them—especially the blackberry in the United Kingdom—are regarded as wild or hedgerow plants, but can make a fine specimen when grown purposefully and trained against a wall. Nurtured in this way, the fruits are bigger, juicier, and sweeter, just as we all remember them from childhood.

Vines (*Vitis vinifera*)

Vines are a real luxury to grow and need to be housed in a glasshouse or tunnel in temperate climates like that of the United Kingdom. I find the dessert varieties absolutely delightful and regularly bountiful too. They do require some skilled understanding if you are to grow and maintain a good harvest, but are worth considering if you have the space. In warmer climates, therefore, the option of making wine is a very real draw, and there are, in fact, many biodynamic wine producers.

Large country garden

Charles Dowding from Somerset, UK, has a large garden with ⅕ acre (800 square meters) under vegetable production. The garden is situated in the Somerset village of Alhampton, in South West England, and has a loam over clay soil with a pH of 7.5.

Charles comes from a farming family. He read geography at university, but, on returning to the family farm after graduating in 1982, he realized that his role in life was to work the land. It was something he had to do. Since then he has been a grower of food, developing a deep knowledge of market gardening.

A gentleman named Charlie Wacher first set him on his current path. From then on his main influences have been books, namely works by the late Lady Eve Balfour and Sir Albert Howard, who were both pioneers of organic farming in the 20th century.

Charles is himself a pioneer of modern growing without soil disturbance, which is recognized as no-dig gardening. He is entirely organic in his methods and believes that you need a deep respect for the soil and its structure. Charles also firmly believes that far fewer weeds grow as a result of disturbing the soil as little as possible. He questions presumptions and traditions, and is always experimenting and seeking better ways of doing things.

Charles treats his garden with the biodynamic preparation BD 500, sensing that it has a great benefit. He sows about 50 per cent of his seeds

A large garden can accommodate different growing environments, and provide food all year round.

following his own interpretation of Maria Thun's calendar, and the remaining crops as and when it is practical. As a result of his own experiences, he believes the full moon has a greater influence than the elemental days.

"I base my life around growing for love and deep pleasure, and a sense of connection with my garden, as well as the satisfaction of growing for people who really appreciate my produce."

A polytunnel is an affordable and productive environment for growing summer and winter long.

∧ Red and white onions grown on the surface of no-dig, organic beds are nearly ready for harvesting.

∨ A mix of food and flower plants in large gardens makes for diversity and attracts a host of beneficial insects.

CHAPTER 5

Growing for Flowers

I love flower gardening and, while I find vegetable gardening rewarding, it is in the flower garden that my heart resides. Ornamental gardens are the most frivolous use of land; they are for pure pleasure and, just like a painting, sculpture, or poem, are created to stimulate a sensory or emotional reaction. Unlike static art, however, flower gardens change daily and need constant work to keep them on track. Ornamental gardens are traditionally more organic than vegetable ones, which is odd considering we don't eat the produce. The sense of organic satisfaction to be gained from them is perhaps weaker, but for me is prevalent in the abundant wildlife and strongest in the biodynamic flower garden. To sit in the sun, admiring borders, while enjoying the hum of bees working, butterflies dancing, and birds singing, is one of the most wholesome of feelings. A biodynamic flower garden is not just a visual work of art; it is the creation of a diverse ecosystem, a patch of natural brilliance.

Perennials

Perennial plants are those that live year after year, and consist mostly of herbaceous plants that die down every winter. They are the muscle of the garden, with trees, shrubs, and hedges being the skeleton. It is possible to have a wonderful display of color from early summer to fall (autumn) using only eight different types of perennial. You only have to tidy them up when they have died back and hoe around them to keep weeds down. The adventurous gardener can play with a vast range of perennials, orchestrating scintillating displays, dramatic color combinations, and architecturally bold schemes.

Crocosmia adds excitement with its hot, fiery flowers, being especially useful in association with blacks, reds, and purples.

Two advantages of growing perennials are that they are usually very hardy and can also tolerate a broad range of soil types. Perennials in my care have tolerated temperatures ranging from 95°F (35°C) down to 5°F (-15°C) in the same year, performing well and with no signs of stress. It is this robust nature that makes perennials so versatile, and allows us to create gardens that endure for years. With good care, mature perennial clumps can be periodically divided into a number of smaller plants, which not only keeps them healthy, but also allows you to move them about and develop your displays.

Sourcing perennials

Perennial plants are available as seed and also small or large potted plants. If you have time, they can be raised very cheaply in large numbers from seed, giving you an opportunity to give them a fully lunar and biodynamic start in life. Similarly, you can buy them as young plants, propagate them by division or from cuttings to increase your stock, and so create a garden over time. If you prefer to buy in young plants, then I suggest sourcing plants that are still small, which will be better value for money. A young plant in a 3½in (9cm) pot, for example, will reach the same size as one grown in a 34-fl-oz (1-liter) pot in only a month—and at half the price. This approach also has the added benefit of bringing as little soil or potting compost into your garden as possible that is not organic.

Using perennials

Gardening well with perennials is rather like watching a water fountain with many jets. In a mixed border, for example, the shrubs provide height and soon the early spring flowers leap up, before falling away again. The next jets of interest appear in the form of perennials as they race upward, some growing faster and flowering first, before falling away in turn to allow others to take central focus. It is like this throughout the flowering season until everything dies back and the dormant shrubs are left to wait out the winter months.

Perennials vary greatly, having different leaf shapes, textures, and colors, and an equally wide range of flowering qualities. Gardens may be designed to be at their best for a fixed period—perhaps as a spring-themed border or high summer area—or they can be skilfully designed to deliver interest all season. Tall spikes, such as foxgloves (*Digitalis*), can be used to set off rounded roses or peonies, while the linear foliage of irises will stand out against geraniums and

< *Allium sphaerocephalon* blends perfectly in this soft grouping of *Gaura* and grasses. The beauty of alliums is that they take up little space.

V Geraniums are star performers in many situations, and a good-value, reliable addition to any perennial border.

lady's mantle (*Alchemilla mollis*). Arranging your garden with variety in mind will result in many layers of interest, with continual textural changes and flowers all season, as well as providing much-needed diversity for wildlife.

In the biodynamic perennial garden, plants grow at Nature's strongest, so it is easy to see why many biodynamic gardeners claim their gardens are more vibrant, the flowers have a deeper, richer color, and the scent is so much stronger than in other gardens. The perennial garden is a very enjoyable place to be and, with such a wide range of wildlife, it feels like a special community.

Top ten perennials

* *Allium*: This range of perennial bulbs is very useful.

* *Aster*: Good for late-season color, especially *A. lateriflorus horizontalis*.

* Day lily (*Hemerocallis*): Reliable perennials for the border.

* *Euphorbia*: This is a huge genus, with many good perennials to choose from. Reliable species include *E. characias*, *E. mellifera*, and *E. x pasteurii*.

* Foxglove (*Digitalis*): Some are biennial and some perennial. Particularly good are *D. ferruginea*, *D. grandiflora*, and *D. lutea*.

* *Geranium*: A wide range of great and reliable performers. *G. psilostemon* is very good.

* Hollyhock (*Alcea*): Specifically *A. rosea*, which is technically a biennial, but often lives longer and seeds easily.

* *Iris germanica* varieties: These have a short flowering season, but are delightful.

* *Knautia macedonica*: Looks lovely in many planting schemes.

* *Verbena bonariensis*: One of my all-time favorite plants. Now quite common, it performs brilliantly all summer, fits in many schemes, and seeds freely.

Annuals

Annuals provide some of my favorite garden flowers, filling me with wonder, pride, and admiration every season. My own garden is never without a variety of *Cosmos bipinnatus* threading through the borders—indeed, I have never tired of its delicate flowers in 15 years of using it. If shrubs and hedges act as the garden's skeleton, and perennials its muscle, then annuals are without doubt the jewelry, makeup, tattooing, and, in some cases, the saucy underwear of the gardening world. While other plants provide consistent displays year after year, being reliable and necessary, it is annuals that provide the excitement, and they can be easily changed and tweaked each year.

Botanically speaking, an annual is a plant that germinates, grows, flowers, seeds, and then dies within one season. Many plants that horticulture defines as annuals are, in fact, tender perennials. These will grow comfortably all year round in their native climate, but are unable to survive the colder winters found elsewhere. Due to their "annual" life cycle, annuals take a little while to reach flowering maturity, but will provide color from mid-summer until they finally succumb to the cold weather.

Designing with annuals

Annuals are excellent plants because they add an extra layer of interest to flower gardens. Their lighter, fast-growing habit makes them ideal for slotting into spaces and threading through an established border. I purposefully leave areas for planting with annuals, perhaps starting the season with tulips, followed by alliums, and then tender annuals. These are an excellent way of following on from early summer plants such as *Iris*, *Delphinium*, *Paeonia*, and *Geranium*, which give a great display early on, but then spend the rest of the season looking like green blobs.

Pots and containers also make good homes for annual plants, and can be used to brighten up dull corners or give great cheer to a front door. The added benefits of growing annuals in containers is that you can move these around, depending on where you want to sit and enjoy them, or position them in a border to make the most of a display.

Selecting annuals

Choosing which annuals to grow will largely depend on what you wish to achieve and where they are to be located. Some annuals are low growing, others trail, and some are tall and vigorous. There are annuals suitable for the vegetable garden or for attracting pollinating insects, while there are others that are purely for display. Trawling through good seed catalogs seeking out unknown plants or new varieties is one of the highlights of a winter's evening. In a world of "instant everything," selecting and ordering seed that has to be germinated first, before flowering weeks or months later, can bring a welcome and restrained calm.

Think carefully about the areas you wish to plant up and make sure you consider each plant's eventual height and spread, as well as its propagation needs if you are growing from seed. Some seeds need heat to get them going and so are best raised in a greenhouse. Others just need an area that is protected from the cold, while some don't tolerate being transplanted and so have to be sown directly in the garden. I tend to select annuals that can be raised in individual cell trays or pots and then planted out, as I prefer not to devote space to raising seed in borders. I also find annuals need a lot of care when young, often being riddled with weed seedlings that cannot be hoed off.

< French marigolds (*Tagetes patula*) are best raised in individual cell trays or pots, and then planted out as young plants.

∧ Californian poppies (*Eschscholzia californica*) do well at the front of a border and are best sown direct, not being suited to transplanting.

Useful tip

If you are following a moon calendar, then choose an appropriate flower day to sow, pot on, and plant out. Try to carry out the last two tasks during a descending moon, which will put the young plants under less stress as they settle in.

Reaching great heights, yellow sunflowers (*Helianthus annuus*), here planted with white *Cosmos*, make a fine, late-summer display and can be grown annually from seed.

Growing annuals

Raising annuals from seed in cell trays is perhaps the most efficient method of growing them. In the past, I have produced thousands of annuals from a small greenhouse and a few coldframes. Indeed, in less than 10 square feet (1 square meter), I can usually raise 50 healthy cosmos for planting out.

The sowing method for annuals is much the same as that for raising vegetable seeds in pots (see pages 88–9). Remember that you should use organic compost for potting and that just prior to a full moon is the best time for sowing. If the cells are larger, say approximately 2in (5cm) square, you can often get away with planting straight out into the garden at this stage without potting on the seedlings into a larger pot first. If this is the case, then make sure there are plenty of roots forming and that the plant easily brings all the potting compost with it when removed from the cell. Personally, I prefer to raise my seedlings in slightly smaller cells and then to bring the young plants on in 3½in (9cm) pots, as this helps them to reach a strong stage for planting out. In the case of cosmos, as well as many other tall annuals, the young plants are less likely to succumb to slugs by this stage or be overshadowed by perennials.

The trick is to get annuals planted out so they don't spend too long in their cells or pots. If they are restricted or short of nutrients, they will struggle to establish themselves well in a border. You also need to avoid planting them out before the last frosts have passed, so pot on rather than neglect them or plant them out too early. (For guidance on planting out annuals, see pages 122–3.)

Top ten annuals

* **Californian poppy (***Eschscholzia californica***):** A bright, warm little plant that seeds about, growing as an annual each season.

* ***Cleome spinosa***: A more recent annual for use in summer borders, providing lovely late season color.

* ***Cosmos***: A real performer from mid-summer through to the first cold frosts. It repeat flowers, adds value to a perennial border, and is good in containers. Several nice color mixes are widely available.

* ***Helichrysum petiolare***: Technically a half-hardy perennial, this lovely gem doesn't make it through United Kingdom winters and is treated as an annual. With its trailing silver foliage, it is fantastic in containers of mixed plantings.

* **Hollyhock (***Alcea rosea***):** Actually a biennial, this flowers, seeds, and dies over two years. It is a star performer in beds and borders.

* ***Lavandula multifida***: A hardy perennial in Mediterranean climates, this soft, light lavender can be used as an edging plant, has gray foliage and lovely blue flowers, and a strong oregano-like scent.

* **Love-in-a-mist (***Nigella damascena***):** An ancient cottage-garden annual that is still widely used due to its simple beauty. It self seeds through the border.

* ***Plectranthus argentatus***: A half-hardy perennial that should be grown as an annual. It has large, silver, nettle-like leaves and is excellent used as part of a container scheme.

* **Sweet pea (***Lathyrus odoratus***):** Another old garden favorite, which is excellent in borders and containers. There are many good varieties to choose from.

* ***Viola***: Very common as winter bedding and great performers. There are some very lovely little varieties available.

Planting Out

Planting a perennial and/or annual border requires the same preparation as for a vegetable garden, with the no-dig approach working well here too. But it is more important that you start out with no nasty weeds, as perennial plants will sit in the same spot for longer than edible crops and are easily invaded by undesirables. A patient approach solves this: prepare the bed well by mulching with cardboard, adding a thick layer of organic matter, and then covering with black plastic for at least one year.

When planting perennials it is easy to put them too close together. Although it is quite natural to want the scheme to look mature as quickly as possible, it takes three growing seasons for perennials to really fill out. A dense initial planting will soon become too dense, with weaker plants having to fight for a spot, and the bed will have a congested and choked feel. You can, of course, use annuals to fill in any unsightly gaps between perennials while these get established.

There are a great many perennials available, so use a reference book to check on eventual heights and spreads to ensure the ones you choose will fit your planting space. Keep the book to hand when planting out to make sure you allow enough space between neighboring specimens so they can reach their eventual size. Planting distances are less critical for annuals because they only usually last for one flowering season before being discarded.

When planning a bed or border filled with perennials and annuals, remember to plant during a descending moon phase, if possible, because a descending moon has less power to draw up sap, which means that the plants will have an easier time taking root. It is also sensible to avoid planting in hot spells, with late winter and early spring being the best times for hardy perennials, as well as tender perennials and annuals (as soon as the risk of cold weather has passed).

< Planting at the right density is important. A mature border will be naturally busy, but annuals can be used to fill in any gaps and provide late interest.

How to plant out

① Planting perennials and annuals in the soil is not difficult, but should be done correctly. I aim to dig a planting hole that is just the right size by using a planting spade for plants in 34fl oz (1 liter) pots and upward and a trowel for those in smaller ones. *As usual, check your moon calendar before planting to be sure that you are working on a flower day.*

② Dig the hole and make sure it is of the right depth—the surface of the potting compost in the pot should be level with the surface of the soil. Many advise teasing out the roots before planting, which apparently speeds up rooting, but I haven't done this for years. Plants aren't silly; they will soon root outward, and teasing out the roots also means breaking them, which causes further stress to the plants.

Supporting taller annuals
Annuals such as *Cosmos*, *Cleome*, and *Nicotiana* may require immediate support with canes or pea sticks if they are planted out late. Lush growth in pots can sometimes be a little too heavy for the plants to stand up alone until they have had time to put down roots.

③ Using the soil you removed when digging the hole, crumble and push it down into the remaining voids, firming in well with your hands. The remaining soil can then be crumbled and scattered about the immediate area.

④ Continue to put in the rest of the plants you selected for the bed or border in the same way, keeping their required planting distances in mind.

⑤ Water in the new plants, and do this frequently unless it has been quite wet. This is necessary because the plants will take a few weeks to root well, even though they are now in the ground. After two weeks you can start reducing the watering, depending on the weather. Annuals can be a little more needy of water, having been used to quite regular watering in a "nursery condition," so keep an eye on them until they are established.

Border Maintenance

Maintaining a planted border is quite straightforward, requiring four main operations: feeding, weeding, supporting, and tidying. Ornamental garden borders should be mulched with well-balanced compost, just like vegetable gardens. The most convenient time to do this is during the winter months, following a good tidy-up. My preference has always been to apply the mulch toward the end of winter before spring growth begins. This not only makes the nutrients available at the start of the season, but looks really smart, too.

Feeding

This should be carried out annually if you have enough organic matter, which is more likely with biodynamic garden compost because it is very potent and provides the most nutrients, meaning that it can be applied more thinly. At the very least, try to vary the material you use, as applying the same compost every year can lead to a build-up of some nutrients and a deficiency in others. In addition to garden compost, the ornamental garden also benefits from applications of BD 500, which will condition the soil further. During the height of the growing season BD 501 can also be sprayed onto plants to aid flowering and seed production.

Weeding

Controlling weeds is important, and best dealt with by regular hoeing. This operation is fast and easy if the weeds are caught young, but be aware of seedlings from annuals that you wish to keep. Favorites such as Verbena bonariensis, for example, will self-seed all over the place, but need to be given time to establish. If you fall foul of time, and the weeds get away, be sure to pull them before they set seed, as this will multiply next year's weed population enormously.

Providing support

If you don't want to go to the trouble of supporting taller plants, then you can select low-maintenance plants with some careful research when planning your garden. If this isn't a concern, and you crave exciting variety, then you may choose plants that need support when growing. Many will become tall and fall under their own weight or due to weather, which can be prevented by staking. A wide range of manufactured plant supports can be purchased, but I like to use pea sticks. Pea sticks are the tips and side twigs of hazel (*Corylus avellana*) or birch (*Betula pendula*), which are harvested in the winter from young coppice growth and woven into frameworks over the plant. The sticks are pushed into the ground and the feathered twigs woven together just above the fresh spring growth. At this stage they look beautiful, and the plant then grows through and hides the framework naturally. It is all a little more effort than using bamboo canes or metal frames, but much more pleasing to the eye and also enjoyable to make.

< Sweet peas (*Lathyrus odoratus*) are climbing up stick supports in this mixed border. Cut in winter, during an ascending moon, the sticks may last several seasons.

∨ Pruned annually, *Buddleia* produces vibrant flowers in abundance, and is very popular with pollinators.

> Well-fed, weed-free soil allows self-seeding plants such as *Verbena bonariensis* to thrive.

Clearing and tidying

As the seasons progress, herbaceous plants grow, flower, seed, and die back at various stages. It will depend on personal preference when you want to tidy them up. Some plants will stand gracefully all winter, looking especially beautiful when covered with frost, while others collapse and look scraggy by mid-summer. How and when you cut the latter back varies, so again I recommend following the advice of a good book. Some herbaceous plants can give you a second show of flowers if treated correctly. When all have withdrawn into the soil, and the tops are ready to be cleared, this enjoyable winter task not only leaves the garden tidy, but also gives a good quantity of fresh material for the compost heap, so don't dispose of it.

Carrying out these simple maintenance stages will help you to keep your ornamental flower garden looking marvelous all year round, as well as teaming with life.

Dead-heading

Dead-heading is an important routine task for maintaining flower production. When a flower is fertilized, it starts to produce seed, which is the ultimate aim of the plant. Removing the "dead heads," or spent flowers, stops the plant producing seed and makes it focus on the production of new flowers instead. To keep a plant flowering until the end of the season, simply snip the stems of dead flowers back to the main stem.

∧ Providing plants for pollinating insects is important. The more interesting your garden, the more diverse this community will be. This is key for pollination and production in vegetable gardens.

Birds, Bees, and Butterflies

Diversity in the garden is of great importance when gardening naturally and the soil must be a welcoming place for as many organisms as possible. However, it doesn't stop there, for everything around us needs to beat with the same pulse. There are two other important roles that the natural world can play in helping the gardener—and these are pest control and pollination.

Pest control

It tends to be the case that for everything that lives, there is something else to eat it. And, at the moment, we humans seem to be at the top of that food chain. Within that chain there are insects that eat or damage plants, which is not good. Fortunately, there are other insects that eat the plant eaters. The first to spring to mind is the ladybug (Coccinalidae family), which is a hungry muncher of aphids. Chemically killing the aphids can mean the same fate for the ladybug, as for most other insects. For this reason, it is essential to garden organically, without chemical pesticides and insecticides, in order to keep the ladybug population thriving in your garden, along with all other beneficial insects.

Birds work in this food chain for us, too. Many species feed on insects during the summer. Birds are especially good for eating caterpillars, slugs, and snails, and on the whole do little damage compared with the benefits they bring. I have already mentioned how to discourage birds from eating fruit (see page 110), and noted that it is often necessary to cover brassicas with mesh to preserve the crop (see page 101). If you take precautions like these, there is plenty of scope for us all to live together.

Our four-legged friends play a role too. Hedgehogs are excellent eaters of slugs and snails, but need careful consideration. Fencing can make passage hard for them, while they also need some suitable places to hide. Cats can help deter rodents, but may not be great for birds, whereas dogs are useful for getting rid of cats (to the amusement of some). Beyond this are the reptiles, with and without legs, which do a superb job against the molluscs, as well as against a range of insects.

If I were a naturalist, I could go on, but this snapshot should show you how a diverse range of wildlife can have an impact. We have to provide suitable habitats, tolerate a little scruffiness in places, and, most of all, be prepared to share a little of our produce. But does it really work? Of this I am 100 per cent certain. Here, in the United Kingdom, I have grown hostas, which are highly prone to slug damage, in woodland settings where the conditions are perfect for pests. There was no damage to any leaf and they were subjects of wonder, without any chemicals having been used at all. The only explanation must have been the birds and frogs that lived there too.

Pollination

Pollination requires the same natural diversity, and without pollinators there would be very little produce. Flowers are visited by a host of insects, such as bees, wasps, hoverflies, beetles, and butterflies. This not only feeds the insect world, but also results in the pollination of much of the plant kingdom. A single bee will visit thousands of flowers, but it will also take poison back to the colony, which is eaten by hundreds. Although we can easily damage the natural cycle, we can just as easily help it. If we provide late-season organic flowers, the colony is more likely to get through the winter, and this is the case for many pollinators. Overall, the answer is obvious: diversity matters, and we can help provide it.

> This beautiful peacock butterfly is enjoying the rich nectar, but its caterpillars live and rely on other plants such as nettles (*Urtica dioica*) and hops *Humulus lupulus*).

Seed Mixes for Wildlife

There is clearly an obvious need to increase the wildlife in our gardens, but how do we go about achieving this? Doing nothing other than gardening biodynamically will soon see change, and in time a wilder habitat will develop, eventually bringing more life with it. You can assist in this process by providing the conditions that are needed through gardening, and a really good way is to sow wildlife seed mixes. These are usually available as either bird-beneficial or insect-and-bee-beneficial blends, but there is room for both.

The plants grown from bird seed mixes are designed to provide the conditions that insects like during spring and summer, with the insects then providing food for young chicks and fledglings. The plants then provide very crucial food in the form of seeds, which remain available throughout the winter months. The seed mixes usually consist of annuals and biennials, giving a broad range of food sources, with varied times of maturity. Seed mixes designed specifically for pollinating insects achieve much the same result, and are often focused on bees. Commonly made up of native wildflowers, these mixes may also contain exotics, all of which are known to provide well for insects throughout the season.

Seed mixes are very specific to continent, country, region, and climate. They will also have certain soil requirements, so it is worth spending some time choosing the right one. The best advice will come from the seed merchants, who should be based in the country or region in which you garden. I strongly suggest you choose the supplier carefully and be certain that they have a long, strong reputation. I was recently advised by Dr. Wolfgang Stuppy, who is a Seed Morphologist at the Kew Millennium Seed Bank, that many wildflower mixes are not what they claim to be. He purchased some economy batches of seed via the Internet, and was shocked to find that they had little or no genuine wildflower content. They consisted mostly of common

< Plants for wild flower meadows can be raised from seed, creating rich and diverse habitats and, in time, even wonderful displays of wild orchids.

commercial annual seed found in gardens, with no guarantee of viability.

Depending on the scale of your gardening, how you raise the seed will vary. On a small scale, many seed suppliers recommend that you germinate the seed traditionally in trays, in which case use individual cell trays. Sowing on a flower day prior to a full moon is the optimum method. The young seedlings should be raised to become healthy plants and then planted either in open soil or lawns. With plenty of watering to get them going, they should then settle in and live healthily. When planting into lawns, I am referring to grass that is being converted to meadow. Wildflowers need to set seed in order to increase, which means not cutting the grass until mid- to late summer, and taking away the "hay" to reduce fertility. Young plants may also struggle if the grass is too fertile. The best way to reduce this fertility is by sowing the hemiparasite yellow rattle (*Rhinanthus minor*), which weakens the grass by feeding from it.

On a large scale, it is better to sow the seed into open ground, which has been prepared especially, and should consist of slow-growing meadow grasses if that is the desired result. You may wish to sow only flowering and seeding plants in a type of natural border or swathe, which will resemble an agricultural field on the very largest of scales, but can look very attractive.

∧ Well-placed shrubs such as this *Buddleia* provide plenty of nectar for visiting insects. The unpopular cabbage white butterfly will in turn feed birds like the common sparrow.

∨ This bumble bee is enjoying the flower of a thistle plant, which can be left to provide valuable food, but then weeded out before it sets seed.

Cutting Flowers for Display

I regard myself as a terrible flower arranger, but was heartened one day when an unarranged bunch that I had delivered to an employer's house was greatly enjoyed as presented. My personal preference is for loose and informal arrangements, gathered from the garden when the flowers are at their best, and popped in a vase to enjoy. I feel such arrangements reflect the garden, of which they are an echo, and bring Nature into the house. I recently had a simple bunch of *Verbena bonariensis* and *Persicaria amplexicaulis* on a windowsill, which was visited by a wide range of bees for several days, and every evening glowed as the sun set behind it.

I tend to make no effort to grow flowers especially for cutting, and cut only what is looking lovely in the moment. However, if you are starting from scratch or have a small garden, and want to have plenty of cut flowers, then it is worth selecting plants well. The two factors to consider are ensuring a long seasonal range of flowers and using plants that flower for a long duration (these are also known as "cut-and-come-again"). The two I have mentioned are very easy to grow and flower for at least three months continually, which makes them ideal for providing flowers. The other end of the spectrum includes plants such as Gladiolus, which produce a spectacular series of blooms on one stem, but only once per season. To have room for this is great, and plants like these are an essential part of a cut-flower border, but they are not the best use of space in a small garden.

Annuals and biennials are also an excellent source of flowers for cutting, being easy and cheap to raise from seed, as well as prolific repeat bloomers. They, along with hardy perennials, will give you a selection of flowers that is far more interesting than the average florist's range. I really like the advice and suggestions given by Sarah Raven (see *Resources*, pages 156–7), who has spent many years writing on this subject and perfecting the art. There are, however, no rules when it comes to cut flowers—just some plants that will last longer and cut well.

Foliage plants

Using foliage plants can be a great way to improve a bouquet, adding structure, providing support, and creating striking visual effects. I like dark foliage with contrasting flowers, such as *Physocarpus* or *Sambucus nigra*, but also the structural green of *Euphorbia*.

A vibrant bowl of sunshine, cut on a flower day and floated in water, these flowers make a perfect table display.

Seasonal flowers for cutting

SPRING
✸ Daffodils (*Narcissus*)
✸ Hellebores/*Helleborus* (using just the flowers floating in water)
✸ *Scilla* (like jewels in tiny vases)
✸ Snowdrops (*Galanthus*)
✸ Wallflowers/*Erysimum* (some are biennial and some perennial)

EARLY SUMMER
✸ *Ammi majus*
✸ *Centaurea*
✸ Foxgloves (*Digitalis*)
✸ Marigolds (*Calendula*)
✸ Poppies (*Papaver*)
✸ Sweet rocket (*Hesperis matronalis*)
✸ *Salvia*
✸ Scabious (*Scabiosa*)
✸ Sweet peas (*Lathyrus odoratus*)

HIGH SUMMER TO FALL (AUTUMN)
✸ *Aster*
✸ *Cosmos bipinnatus*
✸ *Persicaria*
✸ Roses
✸ Sweet peas (*Lathyrus odoratus*)
✸ *Verbena bonariensis*

WINTER
✸ Winter twigs and stems, e.g. *Cornus alba* and *C. stolonifera*, *Corylus avellana* 'Contorta'

NOTE: Remember to cut flowers for display on a flower day, preferably in the morning when the Earth is exhaling.

An unlikely selection, here *Euphorbia*, *Gaura*, umbellifers, and other flowers from the flower border form a simple, energetic arrangement.

Five minutes of careful picking brings various flowers from the garden together so that they can be enjoyed inside as well as out.

Patti O'Brien

Devon Biodynamic Gardens

Patti gardens at home, but also maintains other private gardens biodynamically in the Exeter area of Devon, England. Patti's gardens range in size from 10 x 16ft (3 x 5m) to 2.5 acres (1 hectare), with soils ranging from heavy clay to sandy. The clay is extremely fertile but can also be very wet, whereas the sandy soil is lovely to work but nutrient-poor.

∧ Large or small, Patti's biodynamic gardens are crammed with layers of interest, as well as being full of healthy growth.

This small suburban garden is thriving due to the regular application of biodynamic preparations and principles.

Biodynamic gardeners often notice more intense color in their gardens, as is seen in this fuchsia flower.

"I am better with plants than people, I can feel them and have an intuition."

Patti comes from a long line of skilled gardeners that goes back generations, and feels that gardening is in her genes. After reading modern languages at university, she went on to train in organic agriculture. She then worked at Kites Nest Organic Farm, in Worcestershire, where she experienced working the vegetable garden—and was hooked. Patti has learned further from short courses and garden visiting, as well as creating her own gardens and those for her customers. She has found Geoff Hamilton, Charles Dowding (see pages 112–13), and Laurence Hills to be great influences, along with Lynette West for her biodynamic skills.

Patti is a passionate organic gardener, and is obsessed with compost, which she regards as the place "where life and death join." Her main focus is feeding the compost heap, and she believes the garden radiates from that key focus. She does not use the compost preparations, but sprays BD 500 regularly. When she can, Patti uses BD 501 and finds it very effective for maintaining plant health. Where possible she will always plant under a descending moon, and never works at the moon's perigee. She has noticed that it makes little difference whether she sticks to the elemental days or not.

Patti gardens because she believes it is what she was born to do. She finds biodynamic gardening to be very optimistic, and maintains that: "The farmer and gardener can make it all work better than nature itself."

∧ BD 501 helps with photosynthesis, as well as plant health and vitality, and locks in the sunshine.

∨ Even small spaces can accommodate some different themes. This hot corner relates well to the cool border beyond.

CHAPTER 6

Pots and Containers

There is no need to have a large farm, a garden in the country, or even a sizeable town garden to be biodynamic. You can easily create an oasis that is an attractive haven for life on all scales in a world of concrete. Microorganisms are not aware of your acreage, while insects will enjoy what you grow, preferring the atmosphere that resonates in your tiny urban corner. A bee will fly (3 miles) 5km in search of good nectar and tell all of its friends too, so bringing ever more diversity to your garden. Container growing is versatile, fun, and perfectly suited to many of the small domesticated environments that many of us have as our outdoor space. So, why not go biodynamic on the balcony, and see just how much fragrance, color, and food you can bring to the smallest space?

Biodynamics Anywhere

When Rudolph Steiner first introduced his thoughts on biodynamic agriculture, he only intended to relate the concept only to farming. Nature, however, does not discriminate between farming and gardening, and on a microscopic level cares not whether it is a large, small, or tiny ecosystem. A 10,000 acre (4,000 hectare) farm has the same requirements as a 10 acre (4 hectare) smallholding, and so does a 10in (25cm) pot.

When growing in pots and larger containers, it helps to consider them on a different scale—almost as if they were their own tiny planet. Containers have rigid sides, rather like the bedrock of Earth, as well as soil with its own structure and ecology. They are open to the effects of the cosmos, the pull of the moon, and the weather. Nature will find a way to colonize anything natural—if you leave some fruit to rot on a table at the top of an apartment block, for example, it will soon develop fungi and bacteria, as well as attract flies. Pots on a balcony have far more to offer and, managed biodynamically, will be the best place for life in the area, so you will become known as "the place to be"!

So, how do you go about gardening on a small scale? The following pages will distil all the information in the previous chapters and help you narrow this down to a compact approach suitable for container cultivation. The key principles, however, do not change. The soil needs to be kept in good health, and a wonderful place for plants to be, which is achieved by ensuring that the initial potting media is good, and also through feeding or conditioning with biodynamic preparations.

Research has shown that plants respond to lunar influences even when they are grown in sealed, darkened rooms that have no contact with the atmosphere. Seedlings will most certainly be positively encouraged, wherever you choose to raise them at home, and the daily rhythms of the Earth and moon will not be halted.

There are also other benefits to be gained, in that you will probably have much better control over larger pests, such as slugs and snails, if you are working with containers. By keeping plant growth healthy and plants well fed, you will also have fewer of the smaller bugs and beetles to look out for and deal with.

Growing in pots and containers is not only an excellent way to start gardening, but also a good opportunity to introduce yourself to organic methods, as well as a lunar and biodynamic approach. You can do as much or as little as you have space for, without having to worry about what the rest of the garden is doing.

< Biodynamic principles work whatever the size of growing environment, from prairie to pot, as these strawberries and kumquats show.

The plants in this biodynamic container courtyard still respond to the influences of the moon and grow all the better if biodynamic garden compost and treatments are used.

Selecting Containers

Choosing containers is an important decision and you will need to ensure that certain requirements such as drainage, stability, and breathability are met. I really enjoy finding different containers for growing plants and have sometimes been surprised by what has worked and what has not. There are so many options, whether you are buying new containers, seeking vintage ones, or making them yourself from recycled materials. Above all, choosing containers provides a great opportunity for having fun and creating stylish effects.

Material

I think the choice of container material is important, but note that some of my recommendations are personal preferences. Firstly, it seems only right that if you are trying to garden naturally, then the more natural the container, the better. Stone planters are excellent, but often very large and heavy, whereas clay or earthenware ones are much more manageable. The latter two also breathe, retain moisture, and create good stable conditions, perhaps less so if they are glazed. Metals and plastics are somewhat unnatural, do not breathe, and have no body for providing warmth. I use plastic containers as well as clay ones, but only to bulk up numbers and to house surplus plants. Wooden containers are very nice, too. I find them quite variable, though, depending on how well they drain, but they are, of course, natural.

Size

If space and access are not an issue, then always opt for the biggest containers possible. The larger the container, the more stable an environment it will provide. Larger containers will also stay moist for longer and have good food reserves. The size of container will also depend on your choice of plant. For example, tomatoes do better if they have plenty of rooting space and will get very hungry in a small pot, whereas lettuce for quick use can be grown in more confined containers such as shallow trays, lengths of guttering, or stone troughs. Indeed, many plants do fine in small pots, and these also give you a chance to move things about and refresh what you are growing, so I tend to favor having a range of sizes. When buying containers, always remember to consider their size and weight—will you be able to get them home and will they fit in once you get them there? Quite often, containers can look smaller in a store or market, so be careful.

Old and recycled containers

You can obtain some wonderful old and antique containers, from the basic and functional to the exquisite, stylish, and glamorous. Our gardening forebears were masters at making planters that worked exceptionally well, so old containers are often perfect. Again, be conscious of the material.

< Natural materials make the best containers, especially if you are encouraging natural forces to work in harmony. This willow basket has good airflow and drainage, as well as an attractive and alternative style.

Traditional, fired clay pots give plants perfect growing conditions, having breathable surfaces that retain warmth and good drainage. A more durable investment, always aim for frost-proof options in cold areas.

Large containers provide a more stable growing environment, as the large volume of garden compost contains more nutrients and has better moisture retention. They will also be less vulnerable in challenging weather.

If you have the time, then making your own containers is brilliant fun, and I have seen some wonderful homemade examples. If you are using industrial containers, make sure they haven't had anything nasty in them because this will end up in the potting compost, plants, and potentially in you.

Providing drainage

Always check the drainage in containers. Once, when I was in a hurry, I assumed that the holes in my cell trays were all punched through. However, most weren't and the soil became waterlogged, resulting in the bad germination of some seedlings. Similarly, some converted containers that were formerly water vessels will have holes in them, but these can be too small. Soil life will die if the potting compost becomes waterlogged, and plants will not grow in such a medium, so always remember to check for drainage first.

Potting Compost

As I explained earlier, potting compost is the material you purchase in bags for growing plants in containers (it can also be called potting media). There are so many types of potting compost available that it is impossible to cover everything, so I will try and guide you to making the right decisions.

Manufactured potting compost

Many manufactured potting composts are a blend of materials which are designed to have either multiple uses or perhaps a specific use, such as growing acid-loving plants like heathers and azaleas (this is known as ericaceous potting compost). The quality of the product you use will almost always make a difference, with cheaper composts often being of quite a poor quality in comparison with those from reputable makers.

Modern blended composts contain all sorts of ingredients. These often include recycled materials in an effort to adhere to environmental standards. However, these materials can be unpredictable, so try to use premium products by manufacturers who will have researched and improved on their use. Blended potting composts generally contain some form of feed, while many may also contain pesticides.

Always start with organic potting compost as a base level, but be aware of the ingredients . Most are now peat-free, and some only use region-specific ingredients, and very few contain loam (soil). In large containers with plenty of depth, I actually like a bit of loam to give body, but not too much as it is quite "heavy." I think it's best to avoid anything with added food or fertilizer, unless you know this to be purely organic—based on animal manures, for example.

Using homemade garden compost

①　You will need to sieve home-made compost for potting. Lay a piece of 1in (25mm) wire mesh over a wheelbarrow, shovel the compost on top, and shake it through. Return unsieved material to the heap.

②　The sieved garden compost can be used pure or, as here, blended with 50 percent home-dug loam (soil). Fill the containers for planting with the resulting mix to the level indicated on each container.

③　Planting young plants directly into the compost is an ideal way to get a quick response from seed raised in cells. This salad blend can sit in a corner and will produce leaves within weeks.

Homemade potting compost

Making your own potting compost is the ultimate way to grow in containers. It is all I have done in recent years, but requires a little work and some intuition. I tend to make a cocktail of mixes, depending on what I have available, and then I respond to the growth habits that the plants display (see pages 146–7). The ideal scenario is that I can produce enough garden compost on my compost heap for all of my potting needs, but it takes a little time to get to this stage.

Garden compost must be mature, which means that it has to be fully rotted, dark, and crumbly, with a loamy or woody smell. If left for a year, most compost heaps will be at this stage, but some will get there more quickly. If I am using the garden compost for potting up plants, then I screen it first by laying a piece of 1in (25mm) wire mesh over a wheelbarrow and then shoveling the compost onto the mesh. A little agitation and the fine material falls through, leaving any woody material behind and producing a very nice grade of potting compost.

When I have been short of materials in the past, I have made various potting compost blends until they feel right, having had success with local authority recycled green waste mixed with very well-rotted manure and a little bit of soil for body.

In all cases the nutrient levels in the potting composts will vary, and this needs to be responded to throughout the season by adding liquid organic teas (see page 52–53), biodynamic preparations (see page 54–55), or, if the source material is not biodynamic compost, then you can also mix in the Mausdorf Starter (see page 78).

Homemade garden composts have varying levels of nutrients, and this will be most evident when growing in containers. Keep a close eye on this and apply a feed or treatment at the first signs of deficiencies.

Preparing Containers and Sowing Seed

Getting containers ready for sowing and planting is a really enjoyable and positive task. Containers are rather like small beds in the garden, and each one prepared and set aside is a very measurable, visible result.

Make sure that there is sufficient drainage in containers, but not too much. This example is good and, remember, there is no need to wash out containers. This pot is fine to use as it is.

Container preparation

Having chosen your containers, you will need to ensure they have good drainage before planting them up. Modern, purpose-made containers usually have drainage holes, but modified containers might not. So, how much drainage is needed? It's hard to say, but my feeling is that if 10 per cent of the basal area of the pot is made of holes, then that is adequate. The holes need to be big enough not to clog up, but small enough that the potting compost doesn't wash out—so ranging from the size of a pencil up to an inch. One very large hole is not ideal, but this is often what you find with large fired planters. Due to their size and depth, large planters can manage well on a lower percentage of drainage and also have more stable moisture levels. Draining too quickly is better than too slowly, but ideally there needs to be a nice balance.

Contrary to popular myth, there is no need to add crocks, gravel, or other large objects to the base of the container for drainage. It doesn't provide any benefits at all, and research has, in fact, shown that this can make the drainage worse. However, you might want to put a fine-grade mesh over very large holes to stop the potting compost falling out.

There is no need to wash or sterilize pots or containers; at most you might like to brush them out. You don't sterilize the garden, so why a pot? If you are about to use a large planter, remember

< There is no need to add crocks to the bottom of containers, which can, in fact, make the drainage worse. Good potting compost and drainage holes are all that are needed.

How to sow seed in a container

① Having prepared your container, and dealt with the drainage, start filling it with potting compost, gently firming this down as you go. There is no need to force the compost in, as you are just helping it settle. Many pots have a rim around the top, so fill the compost to the line marked by this rim. Leaving a space between the top of the pot and the compost allows water to settle and soak in slowly, rather than pouring over the sides. As a general guide, in a large container or anything without a rim, leave at least an inch at the top without compost.

② Depending on the seed being sown, make little drills for sowing or holes with your finger for larger seed. If you are using homemade compost, some weed seeds will also germinate. For this reason, it is worth sowing the seed in obvious drills or concentric rings, as you can more easily identify what is what later—the seedlings will all look the same as they grow, so anything following a pattern will be what you sowed intentionally.

③ *Remember to check your moon calendar for when to sow and bear in mind that the best time for germination is a few days before a full moon. Sow quite thinly to avoid having to thin the seedlings later on and so that the plants won't be too dense. Cover over the seed with more potting mix, note the sowing date and varieties on a plant label, and water in. Use a watering can with a rose attachment, or a sprinkler, applying a light dose several times so that you don't wash the seed over the edge or around the pot.*

that it will be very heavy once it is filled with potting compost, so prepare and plant in the spot where you are going to place it.

Sowing seed

It is possible to sow directly into pots and containers, just as for sowing seed direct in open beds in the garden. The advantage of doing this is that there is no intermediate stage of raising the seed in cell trays first before planting the young plants in their containers. On the other hand, it does narrow down the range of plants that can be grown throughout a season, which is of particular relevance if you are growing food.

Planting Containers

Planting up containers is an instant-impact and satisfying task, allowing you to fill a dull corner with color or change your living environment both quickly and frequently. As a gardener, I always enjoy that time of year when the frosts are over, early summer has set in nicely, and it's time to plant my pots with summer schemes.

< Container-grown plants can be stored in a "nursery" area and then brought to a prime position when in full flower, as with these lovely dwarf hydrangeas. This allows for rapid changes and great flexibility in your plant displays.

Containers can be used for instant impact in a dull or problem corner. Here, bay laurel (*Laurus nobilis*) has been used to provide privacy on a window balcony.

The initial preparations for planting containers are much the same as for sowing seed: you must ensure good drainage and then fill the container with potting compost, gently firming it in as you go. When planting up, however, you need to allow a little more space for the plants, so don't add potting compost as close to the top of the container as when you are sowing seed.

The key point with planting is to ensure that the final planting depth is correct, in that the surface level of the compost on the young plant needs to end up at the same final level as the surface of the potting compost in the container. If you are leaving a 1in (2.5cm) depression in the container for watering, then this is the level to which you need to plant.

Purchased organic compost will be short on activity from microorganisms, whereas homemade compost will already be healthy and vibrant. It is of further benefit to add Mausdorf Starter when filling the container initially, or to work in some precious biodynamic garden compost. You may, of course, be lucky enough to have produced enough biodynamic compost to fill the container, in which case your plants will enjoy the best possible growing conditions.

Useful tip

The ideal time for adding any plant supports is just after you have planted up a container. For example, if you are planting sweet peas (*Lathyrus odoratus*), then they will need something to climb up. By putting the climbing framework in now, they will latch on quickly and race away, which is better than this being a reactive task and left a little too late.

Planting a "salad bowl" container

① Fill the container with your chosen potting compost, lightly firming it as you go, to the level indicated by the planting rim.

② *Remember to check your moon calendar for when to plant. The best time for planting is in a descending moon on a leaf day for these salad crops.* Remove the first young plant from its pot or tray, and place it in the container to gauge the depth.

③ There is no need to tease out the roots, especially if the young plant is being transplanted at the right time. Teasing out only damages the roots further and increases the stress experienced by the plant.

④ Position the first plant so that its soil level sits at the intended finished compost level in the container. If you plant too deeply, then the plant will rot and die; too shallow, and the result will be instability and root exposure.

⑤ Plant the container with more plants, either building up or removing more potting compost below and around them to ensure that they will be at the right level.

⑥ Continue in this way with the remainder of the plants, adding or removing potting compost to achieve the correct surface level. Gently firming in while you do this ensures the plants will be unlikely to slump.

⑦ Once the plants are in, give them a good drink, filling the container to the brim and letting the water soak through. That alone should be enough and will also settle any last soft spots in the compost. Once the water has soaked in, fill in any areas that have slumped with more compost.

⑧ Three weeks later and the salad plants have filled out nicely. If you pick the outer leaves from the base frequently, then the plants won't become too dense and will provide for a month. *Remember to pick salads leaves in the morning for better vitality and storage.*

Good Combinations in Containers

What to grow in your containers will largely be determined by your personal tastes and needs. There really are no rules here: you will simply be restricted in what you can grow by the requirements of the plant and the space you have available for gardening.

I prefer to keep what I grow for food separate from my decorative containers so that I can plant the food crops successively throughout the season, but this isn't necessary. Containers can be planted very thickly, at a much greater density than in the garden, although you will have to provide more water and food. Try also to balance the requirements of the plant combinations—for example, something leafy with something fruity or flowery—and this will balance out the draw on food reserves a little. The same approach can also be taken for growing habit: so combine something that races up with something that tumbles down, and also perhaps include a mid-range option. That said, it is both simple and elegant to opt for only one type of plant or to repeat the same plants in several containers. As I said, there are no real rules.

< There really are no rules on what to grow in containers, and using different types of pots and baskets adds variety to your display.

Some planting ideas for containers

❋ Tomatoes with either flat-leaved parsley, basil, or French marigolds (*Tagetes patula*).

❋ Sweet peas (*Lathyrus odoratus*) with strawberries in a large, deep container. Plant the sweet peas in the center and the strawberries at the edge to trail down.

❋ *Cosmos bipinnatus* with *Helichrysum petiolare* and ornamental bacopa (*Chaenostoma cordatum*) is good fun, especially if you choose only white varieties of these plants to create a stunning silver and white display

❋ Nasturtium (*Tropaeolum majus*) with pot marigolds (*Calendula officinalis*), some purple *Verbena* such as 'Homestead Purple', and a purple-leaved canna. Plant the nasturtium at the front, with the marigolds and verbena next, and the canna at the center or rear. If the container is large enough, you can have even more fun by planting runner beans at the rear and sending them up a frame or wall.

❋ If you have a gazebo that needs softening, try placing large containers at each corner and plant a runner bean and sweet pea (*Lathyrus odoratus*) in each container. This combination will provide great scent, cut flowers, shade, and food, as well as attract lots of pollinators to pollinate the runner beans.

Planting a wooden trough

1. Add potting compost to the trough; it is a good idea to use a rich, heavier, loamy mix in a large container such as this. The potting compost used here is a blend of manure and loam with a topping of commercial garden compost.

2. *Remember to check your moon calendar for when to plant and bear in mind that the best time for planting is during a descending moon (on a flower day for these flowering plants).* Conscious of the final scheme or layout, plant the first young plant—here a sweet pea (*Lathyrus odoratus*)—in the center of the trough at the correct depth.

3. Continue adding more plants—here, a group of three *Cosmos* followed the sweet pea.

4. As you add further plants, provide enough space around each one. Containers are fun when crammed and overflowing, but you need to allow for subsequent growth.

5. As you plant the trough, continually adjust the level of the potting compost, removing or adding more if required.

6. The trough is now planted, allowing ample room for further growth. It may look at little sparse, but within a few weeks it will be full and flowering away.

< A selection of regularly used herbs is easy to grow in a container by the kitchen door, and tastier than any you can buy. Easier to keep healthy than is often believed, they suit a biodynamic approach, and will reward vigorously.

Growing Herbs in Containers

Herbs grow well in containers and often thrive in the controlled environment they provide. You can also keep herb containers by the kitchen door for convenience and easily replace them if they get tired. Why not plant the herbs you use most in the kitchen in a container and save yourself the expense of buying them?

The term "herb" covers a wide range of plants. This not only includes herbs used every day in the kitchen, but also those that have a useful purpose, rather than being purely ornamental. Fortunately, the majority of them can be grown in containers, which makes it possible to have a very exciting herb garden that is completely mobile. Larger specimens such as bay, rosemary, sage, and lavender can be placed near doors, paths, and seating areas, releasing their scent when you brush against them. Pelargoniums, salvias, alliums, calendula, and nasturtiums are just some of the herbs that can be used for floral interest, while unusual features can also be provided by plants such as hops (*Humulus lupulus*), which are used to make beer and can be grown over a framework to create height and shade.

Most herbs are tolerant of a range of conditions, but it is worth taking a moment to plan your containers and give them the best possible growing environment. If you are growing herbs in individual containers, then you can be quite specific about how they are cultivated, whereas if you are grouping plants together, it is good to match their requirements. To give an example: parsley, chives, and even sage will enjoy a rich, moist container and reward you with continual lush growth. Basil, rosemary, and thyme prefer conditions to be on the dry side and flourish in a heavier, loamy, but free-draining soil. In both cases, they would do well in sun, but if you had to choose, then the first group could tolerate light shade, while the second group would only thrive in full sun. The advantage of container-growing is that things can be moved around, giving plants a few days in the sun to perk up, or moving them into a corner when they are past their best, making the whole scheme quite versatile.

There is a misconception that all herbs need poor, dry conditions. However, they are often left to dehydrate, without sufficient nutrients, and in poor health. By following the advice on container selection, potting media, planting, watering, and feeding, you will be able to give them the correct growing conditions. It's true that some can be a little tricky, but if the potting compost is fresh and of good quality, then it is often the location and conditions that need addressing. If you experience problems, first check the compost by pushing your finger in deep: if it is quite wet, then move the container to a bright location to dry out a little. If the reverse is true, and the container is very dry, then place the container in a bucket or bowl and soak it for a while, as very dry potting compost can struggle to rehydrate. You should also check the location of the container: is it too hot, drafty, and cold or in need of some humidity?

In limiting yourself to growing herbs, you can create a lovely small garden or courtyard, which is of interest all year. It will also provide you with flavors to eat, scents to enjoy, and perhaps the ingredients for creams, soaps, and oils, too.

Planting a simple herb box

① Choose a suitable container. I like this wooden gin crate, which has drainage holes and is easy to move about.

② Fill the container with good potting compost, in this case homemade garden compost from a biodynamic heap.

③ *Check the planting conditions, aiming to plant in a descending and/or waxing moon phase, and on a leaf day for optimum conditions. These first two lunar phases are the most important, as they ensure minimum moisture stress to the plant when it is starting to take root.*

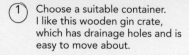

④ Plant the young herbs, spacing them out to allow for growth and ensuring that the final planting depth of each plant is the same as its original potted depth. This selection includes thyme, rosemary, purple sage, and golden oregano.

⑤ Water the plants in and place the crate in a nice, sunny location, which all of these herbs will enjoy. The herbs will eventually need more room, so, when they have been trimmed for a season for use in the kitchen, find a place in the garden for them or transplant them into larger containers.

Container Care

You will need to keep a close and regular eye on plants grown in pots and containers, as the margin for error is much smaller. In a garden setting, you have the luxury of a more stable environment, which means that nutrient deficiencies and drought take a little longer to have an impact, whereas in a small environment, where demands on available resources are high, conditions can change within hours.

∨ Keeping container-grown plants moist is the most important task to ensure their health and wellbeing. Water late afternoon and evening for the best soil absorption.

Watering

The first routine at which you'll need to become proficient is watering. Young plants will settle in quickly, and will have fewer demands than established ones, but a hot day is still a hot day, and this is where the greatest vigilance is needed. Potting compost must also not sit wet for long periods or anaerobic conditions will develop, killing good soil life and plant roots, as well as introducing bad pathogens. It is fine to soak a pot, but it may not need watering every day. The best way to tell if you need to water is to stick your whole finger in the potting compost. If this is still fairly wet, then don't water. You will learn to judge this based on the season, the planting scheme and your compost, so ensure you provide enough water to get a plant through a hot day. A wilting plant will become stressed, which will make it vulnerable to pests and disease, so keep the conditions healthy.

Feeding

Next you need to keep an eye on feeding and nutrient levels. Instinct should help here, so if a plant is green and healthy, but then starts to look yellow, slow down; if it has dark leaf veins but pale leaves, then it is getting hungry. This is where compost teas come into their own: they are a quick

Feeding with organic tea

(1) This 10-day-old organic tea, made from stinging nettles (*Urtica dioica*), having been sieved of all decomposing remains, is added to a watering can and diluted at a ratio of 10:1 for use as a regular feed.

(2) Apply the feed, allowing it to be absorbed and making sure it doesn't gush over the sides. *The best time to water is late afternoon/evening, with the optimum time being during a descending moon, when the soil inhales and absorbs best.*

way to improve the situation and then you need maintain the nutrient levels going forward. Organic teas take a while to make, usually three to ten days, so being aware of the feeding situation in your containers will help here. Plants take longer to use up the nutrients in large containers and, with a good potting compost, may last all summer, but smaller ones will burn out quickly with lush growth.

Other tasks

Throughout the season tend your potted plants, being sure to remove overcrowded sections or whole plants if required. If the planting is too dense and you get a wet spell, this can allow fungal growth to develop, so try to keep some air movement going. Remove the "dead heads" (spent flower heads that have finished) on decorative plants on a regular basis, otherwise the plant's energy will be put into making seed and not more flowers.

As plants grow, they may need some support, so be aware of this and try to provide it before they fall over. Tall plants, such as sweet peas (*Lathyrus odoratus*) and runner beans, are also better attached to a wall or structure, because the potting compost is often not firm enough to hold supports well. Also remember that tall plants may be prone to blowing over in high winds.

When it comes to emptying containers at the end of the season, don't discard the potting compost, but put it on your compost heap instead. In a very large container, you can happily get away with removing only the top 12–18in (30–45cm), leaving the rest of the potting compost in the container and refilling with fresh potting compost when it comes to planting it again.

The golden rule with containers is to provide care on a little-and-often basis. In this way you will spot things before they become problems and make life easier for yourself.

∧ Regularly dead-head ornamental plants, daily if possible, as this will ensure that their energies go into the production of more flowers rather than seeds.

∨ With regular care and attention, as well as routine feeding, container plants will remain healthy and vibrant throughout the growing season.

A Courtyard Garden

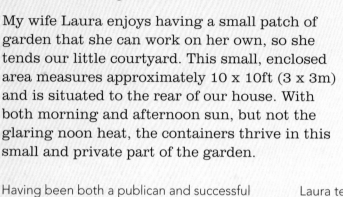

My wife Laura enjoys having a small patch of garden that she can work on her own, so she tends our little courtyard. This small, enclosed area measures approximately 10 x 10ft (3 x 3m) and is situated to the rear of our house. With both morning and afternoon sun, but not the glaring noon heat, the containers thrive in this small and private part of the garden.

Having been both a publican and successful retailer, as well as widely traveled, Laura now runs her own business from home making alternative children's clothing. A natural creative talent, she has no training in horticulture and has learned what she needs from me and by flicking through magazines and books over coffee. She is typical of many owners of small gardens, balconies, and courtyard areas, who learn through trial and error as they go along.

Laura tends this area as a way to shift her focus away from work and likes to step out of the door and spend a few minutes dead-heading, picking tomatoes, weeding, and generally caring for the containers. She finds this is a perfect way to let go of stresses, giving her an opportunity to spend 15 or 20 minutes daydreaming in order to recover her thoughts and settle her mind. As a mother of two young children, this time has the same benefits, although the courtyard is also a

Crammed with food and flowers, this tiny space has a wide range of biodynamic plants, and is a vibrant habitat.

good place for her to sit with them and relax, as well as to watch and learn about Nature.

The containers are filled with homemade organic compost blended with very old manure. They have been planted and tended following the lunar calendar and the elemental days, where possible, and have performed very well. This small area has provided salad leaves, tomatoes, herbs, potted flowers, and cut flowers for the house. The large container also acts as a light screen that provides privacy from the house opposite and from our parking area. Laura values her garden as a place where she can reflect, sit and relax, and spend time with her family. This small area gives her all these things and is a source of happiness and contentment. She also values and respects the natural world, and cares greatly about the origins of her food. To have a small space in which she can realistically achieve these aims is a source of continual happiness.

∧ In small spaces individual blooms become emphasized and valued, like this intense Cosmos flower.

∧ Packed with flowering annuals, this planter provides an effective screen and makes the courtyard private.

> Seated low in a chair, you become immersed in a riot of bold colors and the hum of the insects.

"I love to be outdoors, surrounded by beauty and Nature, and find the haven of my garden provides this. Most of all, it is important that I can share that love and awareness with my children at every opportunity."

Conclusion

My first year as a biodynamic gardener has been both fascinating and challenging, but I know that it is only the beginning of a long journey.

I grew up on a small mixed farm and have been gardening and working the land for just over a quarter of a century. In recent years, I have been completely organic in my approach and feel that I have a strong and intuitive understanding of the natural world around me.

While adopting a biodynamic system in my garden, I have made every effort to follow a lunar calendar by keeping to the phases of the moon, the moon's path, and the elemental days. I have also used biodynamic methods for soil care and plant husbandry, and have not applied a single unnatural additive to my garden.

During my first season gardening biodynamically, I have produced my best vegetables to date: rich, robust and yet delicate, and tasty. I have had little trouble with pests and have lost very few plants to slugs and snails, in spite of a huge number of these troublesome molluscs. I have seen very rapid germination and growth from seeds sown close to a full moon and less from those that are not. I am aware that during ascending and descending moons there are different weather patterns, as well as varying effects on how wet the land lies and on mollusc activity. I plan to continue biodynamic gardening by following its sound husbandry advice, using the biodynamic preparations, and following the phases and path of the moon, but not the elemental days. In time, I may change my view, but for now that is my personal interpretation.

It has been a very interesting process, in which I have definitely become much more aware of everything that goes on around me. I know what the moon is up to, notice the weather more acutely, and see the condition of plants in a more perceptive way. I am also a more relaxed person, with an acceptance that some things go my way, while some don't—and not just in the garden.

There are some fantastic biodynamic farms and gardens, both in the United Kingdom and elsewhere, which are living proof that lunar and biodynamic gardening are not just concepts. To see such health, happiness, and balance in plants, animals, and humans is a rare thing, but something that you can instinctively sense. I urge you to visit these farms and gardens in order to see for yourself the difference a lunar and biodynamic approach can make (see Resources, pages 156–157).

During the course of my research, I have also spoken to many people and found that there is no one prescribed approach to biodynamic husbandry. The most experienced and qualified Steiner acolytes debate constantly, some of them believing that the astronomy element is wrong and that biodynamics is simply about good husbandry, while others wholeheartedly believe in the influence of the elemental days. There is no doubt that it is a very personal thing, and that it must work for you.

I firmly believe that biodynamic husbandry is the best way to work your land and urge everybody who shows an interest to try it—you'll be amazed at the difference it can make to both the edible and ornamental garden, as well as to your life.

Resources

UK (some ship worldwide)

Matt Jackson–Black Sheep Gardens & Landscapes—Garden design with a specialism in vegetable gardens and Arts & Crafts ornamental gardens; advice and consultation www.blacksheepconsultants.co.uk

The Biodynamic Association UK—Resource centre, Seeds, Preparations, Training, Literature www.biodynamic.org.uk

The Biodynamic Agricultural College—Training www.bdacollege.org.uk

Calendars—'The Maria Thun Biodynamic calendar' by Mathias Thun; 'Gardening and planting by the moon' by Nick Kollerstrom

Charles Dowding—Training, advice, consultation and excellent literature on organic, no-dig gardening www.charlesdowding.co.uk

Hazelrowan Wood—Advice & consultation on low impact, sustainable vegetable gardens (home & market) and off-grid sustainable living, South West UK hazelrowanwood@gmail.com

Implementations—suppliers of copper tools, ideal for natural gardening and of top quality www.implementations.co.uk

Lunar organics—Calendars, publications and seeds www.lunarorganics.com

Tamar Organics—organic seed and garden supplies www.tamarorganics.co.uk

Stormy Hall Seeds—biodynamic seed www.stormy-hall-seeds.co.uk UK Biodynamic Farms

USA

Biodynamic Association—Resource centre, Training, preparations, literature, community www.biodynamics.com

Rare Seeds—Organic Heirloom Seeds and supplies www.rareseeds.com

Seeds of Change—organic seeds and supplies www.seedsorchange.com

Josephine Porter Institute—Education, literature and preparations www.jpibiodynamics.org

Reading

The Moon Gardener; A biodynamic Guide to Getting the Best from Your Garden by Peter Berg and Matthew Barton

Gardening and Planting by the Moon by Nick Kollerstrom (updated annually with a calendar)

Rudolph Steiner
–Agriculture Course; The Birth of the Biodynamic method
– Agriculture
–What is Biodynamics? A way to heal and revitalise the Earth

UK Farms

The Blackthorn Trust, biodynamic market garden, Kent www.blackthorntrust.co.uk

Fern Verrow, Herefordshire www.fernverrow.com

Laverstoke Park, Hampshire www.laverstokepark.co.uk

Old Plaw Hatch & Tablehurst Farms, Sussex www.tablehurstandplawhatch.co.uk

Shire Farm, Lincolnshire www.shirefarm.co.uk

Woodlands farm, Lincolshire www.woddlandsfarm.co.uk

Find a biodynamic farm at www.biodynamic.org.uk/links

US Farms

Find a biodynamic farm in your region at www.biodynamics.com

Gardening for Life; The Biodynamic Way by Maria Thun

The Biodynamic Year; Increasing Yield, Quality and Flavour by Maria Thun and Matthew Barton

Biodynamic Gardening; For Health and Taste by Hilary Wright

Index

Author's Acknowledgments

Thanks first and foremost to the Jackson girls: Laura, Rosa, Cicely, and Tilia for your support and patience as I disappeared and tapped away by lamplight.

To Alexandra Iron for setting me on the path of writing, and always helping me in the right direction.

To Posy Gentles for your support and advice along the way. To Caroline West for knowing my work so well, and guiding me through.

To Dan, Patti, Charles, Kate, and Rob who have allowed their precious gardens to be featured, spent time talking to me and sharing some very personal thoughts and feelings, and have been entirely supportive.

To David Merewether for capturing the life and vibrancy of the gardens behind the shutter.

To the team at Tablehurst Farm who, without knowing, opened my eyes to a new way of gardening and living.

Thanks to Cindy Richards and CICO Books for having faith in me.